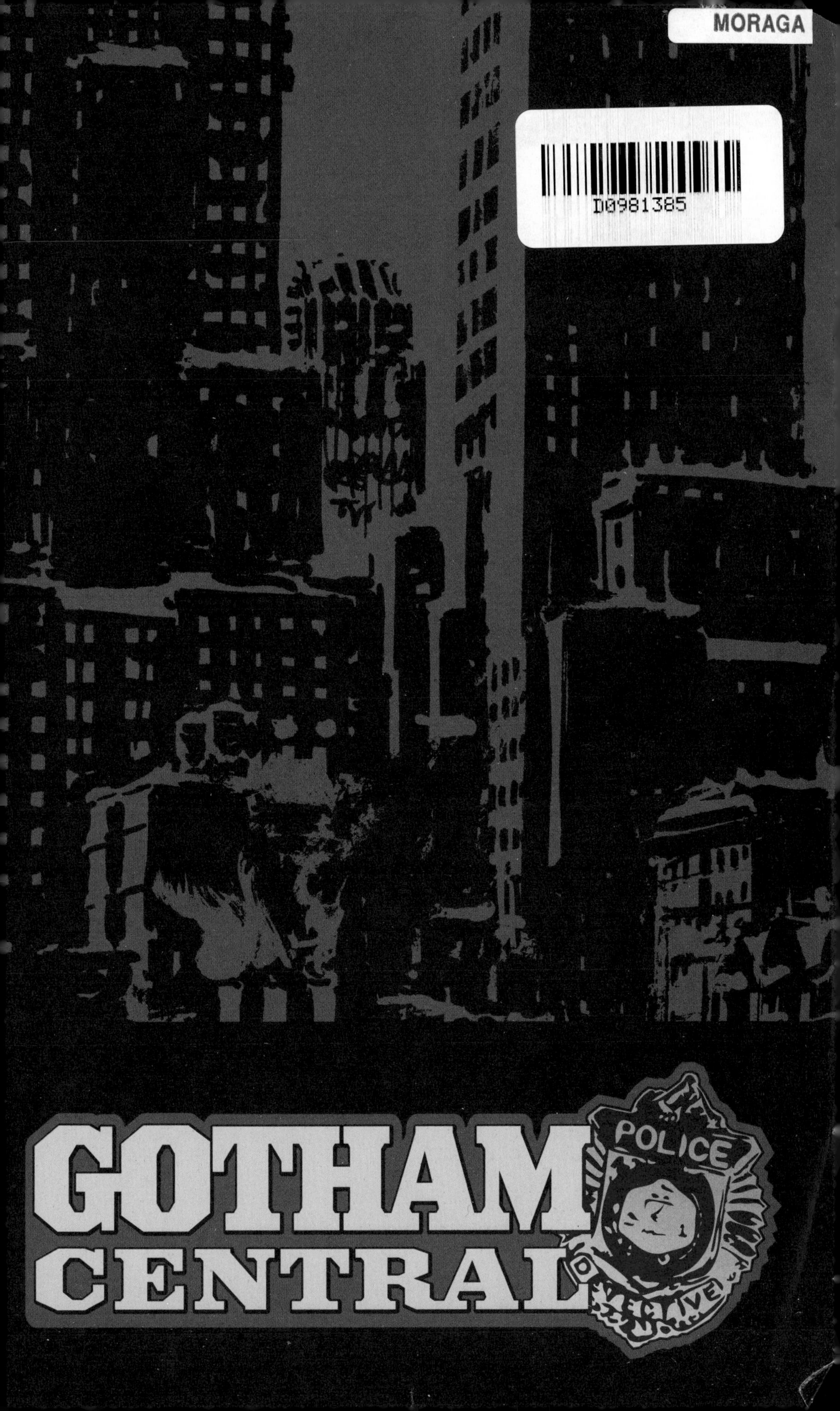
GOTHAM
CENTRAL
POLICE

Dan DiDio VP-EXECUTIVE EDITOR • Matt Idelson EDITOR - ORIGINAL SERIES • Nachie Castro ASSISTANT EDITOR - ORIGINAL SER
Robert Greenberger SENIOR EDITOR - COLLECTED EDITION • Amie Brockway-Metcalf ART DIRECTOR • Paul Levitz PRESIDEN
PUBLISHER • Georg Brewer VP-DESIGN & RETAIL PRODUCT DEVELOPMENT • Richard Bruning SENIOR VP-CREATIVE DIRECT
Patrick Caldon SENIOR VP-FINANCE & OPERATIONS • Chris Caramalis VP-FINANCE • Terri Cunningham VP-MANAGING EDIT
Alison Gill VP-MANUFACTURING • Rich Johnson VP-BOOK TRADE SALES • Hank Kanalz VP-GENERAL MANAGER, WILDSTO
Lillian Laserson SENIOR VP & GENERAL COUNSEL • Jim Lee EDITORIAL DIRECTOR – WILDSTORM • David McKillips VP-ADVERTISI
& CUSTOM PUBLISHING • John Nee VP-BUSINESS DEVELOPMENT • Gregory Noveck SENIOR VP-CREATIVE AFFAIRS • Cheryl Rub
SENIOR VP-BRAND MANAGEMENT • Bob Wayne VP-SALES & MARKETING

GOTHAM CENTRAL: IN THE LINE OF DUTY

COVER ILLUSTRATION BY Michael Lark • COVER COLORED BY Lee Loughridge • GOTHAM SKYLINE INKED BY Stefano Gaudiar

GREG RUCKA & ED BRUBAKER WRITERS

MICHAEL LARK ARTIST & ORIGINAL COVERS

NOELLE GIDDINGS COLORIST

WILLIE SCHUBERT LETTERER

BATMAN CREATED BY **BOB KANE**

THE MEAN STREETS OF GOTHAM

BY LAWRENCE BLOCK

We always knew they meant New York.

Oh, sure, they called it Gotham City. That's where the Bat Signal hung in the night sky like the moon, and where the Batmobile never had to circle the block looking for a parking space. Gotham was home to the Joker and the Riddler and the Penguin, and in its streets and upon its rooftops Batman and Robin the Boy Wonder waged their endless noble battle against the forces of evil.

That was Gotham City, all right, and that was a perfectly fine thing to call it in the alternate universe of comic book fiction. But we're not dim. We knew well and good what town we were talking about, whatever name they fastened on it, and whatever they called its streets and news-papers and citizens.

They were talking about New York.

I mean, why else call it Gotham?

The original Gotham, it may interest you to know, was in England, a village in Nottinghamshire. The name meant "goat town" in Anglo-Saxon, which would seem to suggest that some of the inhabitants kept goats and didn't care who knew it. Back in the thirteenth century, the Gothamites earned a reputation as "wise fools" by feigning insanity in order to avoid paying taxes to King John. (There was evidently something about King John that put people's backs up; it was he, you'll recall, who in 1215 inspired the peers of the realm to force upon him the Magna Carta, that Great Charter that stands as the foundation of all our freedoms, granting the citizenry such rights as trial by jury. But I digress. . .)

King John had long since gone to his reward when the Dutch bought the island of Manhattan and founded a town they called New Amsterdam. And it was almost two centuries after that, in 1807, when Washington Irving published a series of essays entitled *Salmagundi, or the Whims and Opinions of Launcelot Langstaff and Others*,

wherein he referred to the city as Gotham. Irving's use of the name implied that Gothamites were self-important and foolish, but the name shrugged off its connotations and endured.

And wasn't Washington Irving the lad for naming things? *Salmagundi*, which he seems to have cobbled up out of a handful of leftover Scrabble letters, became the name of an artists' club; founded in 1871, it endures to this day, and its brownstone clubhouse boasts the only remain-ing stoop on Fifth Avenue. Meanwhile, Irving fol-lowed *Salmagundi* with *A History of New York*, which he wrote under the pen name of Diedrich Knickerbocker, ostensibly an embittered old codger of Dutch extraction. There's another name that's hung on, and you'll find it attached to any number of present-day New York institutions, including a group of tallish fellows who pass the time throwing a round ball through a hoop. But there I go, digressing again. . .

In 1844, Edgar Allan Poe wrote a series of satirical reports on daily life in New York, which he called Doings of Gotham. (He lived at various New York locations — in Greenwich Village, on West 84th Street, and in a cottage in the Bronx that survives to this day as an Edgar Allan Poe museum.) The author of "The Raven" doesn't seem to have found New York's streets all that mean, but did trouble to call them "with rare exception, insufferably dirty." He went on to lament the $50,000 spent annually for street cleaning, and proposed a novel alternative: "Contractors might pay roundly for the privilege of cleaning the streets, receiving the sweepings for their perquisite, and find themselves great gainers by the arrangement. In any large city, a company of market gardeners would be induced to accept a contract of this character."

Believe it or not, Poe's notion never did reach the right ears, and to this day the city actually spends money to clean the streets. In some years the tab runs even higher than $50,000.

William Sydney Porter, whom you'd know as O. Henry, lived in New York from 1902 until his death in 1910. Many of his stories, especially those in *The Four Million*, were set in New York, but when he called the place Gotham he was just using a sobriquet that had long since been incorporated into the local language. He had other names he invented for the city, most notable "Baghdad-on-the-Subway." Now there's a phrase that must have resonated very differently a century ago than it does today.

●●●●●

Forget the name. Suppose they called the city something else, or nothing at all. Could it be any place but New York?

In 1939, when Bob Kane started drawing BATMAN, the urban landscape alone could have told us what town he had in mind. The high-rises and skyscrapers defined New York in an era where not all that many cities boasted a building much taller than the local water tower.

Things are a little different now, and you don't have to look all that far to find a one-horse town with a genuine skyline. But it's not just the height of the buildings that makes New York the right setting for Batman, and the perfect home for these Gotham cops — dressed, I don't doubt, in GCPD Blue — who fight the good fight in these pages.

It's not the actual meanness of the streets, either. New York, its image notwithstanding, has a lower crime rate than most of the rest of the country, and one that continues to drop. Gentrification has upgraded Harlem and made the Lower East Side unrecognizable, and you pretty much have to leave Manhattan and do some real searching to find a genuinely bad neighborhood these days.

So it's not the crime rate, and it's not the tall buildings. What is it? The answer's somewhere in the following gag:

Tourist to New Yorker: Can you tell me how to get to the Empire State Building, or should I just go #%@&#!!! myself?

The New York energy goes beyond anything you'll find anywhere else. It's too much for some people and it grinds them down, but it lifts up and animates the rest of us.

It gives us the New York edge, which is attitude and something more. Reggie Jackson, who had some of his best years at that ballpark in the Bronx, smiled when someone asked him how he felt about the city. "If you give a New Yorker the first line," he said, "he's got the whole page."

Hey, get a grip, will you? Can you imagine the Joker trying to make his bones by putting one over on the cops in Albuquerque? Or the Riddler trying out conundrums on Fargo's Finest? Can you picture Catwoman in Cleveland, or the Penguin in Peoria, or Two-Face in the Twin Cities? Or our *villain du jour,* the chilling Mr. Freeze, in, say, Fresno?

I didn't think so.

It's Gotham City, baby. Get used to it.

Lawrence Block's novels range from the urban noir of Matthew Scudder to the urbane effervescence of Bernie Rhodenbarr, while other characters include the globe-trotting insomniac Evan Tanner and the introspective assassin Keller. He has published articles and short fiction in American Heritage, Redbook, Playboy, Cosmopolitan, GQ, *and* The New York Times, *and 84 of his short stories have been collected in* Enough Rope. *Larry is a Grand Master of Mystery Writers of America, and a past president of both MWA and the Private Eye Writers of America. He has won the Edgar and Shamus awards four times each and the Japanese Maltese Falcon award twice, as well as the Nero Wolfe and Philip Marlowe awards, and, most recently, a Life Achievement award from the Private Eye Writers of America. In France, he has been proclaimed a Grand Maitre du Roman Noir and has twice been awarded the Societe 813 trophy. Larry and his wife Lynne are enthusiastic New Yorkers and relentless world travelers.*

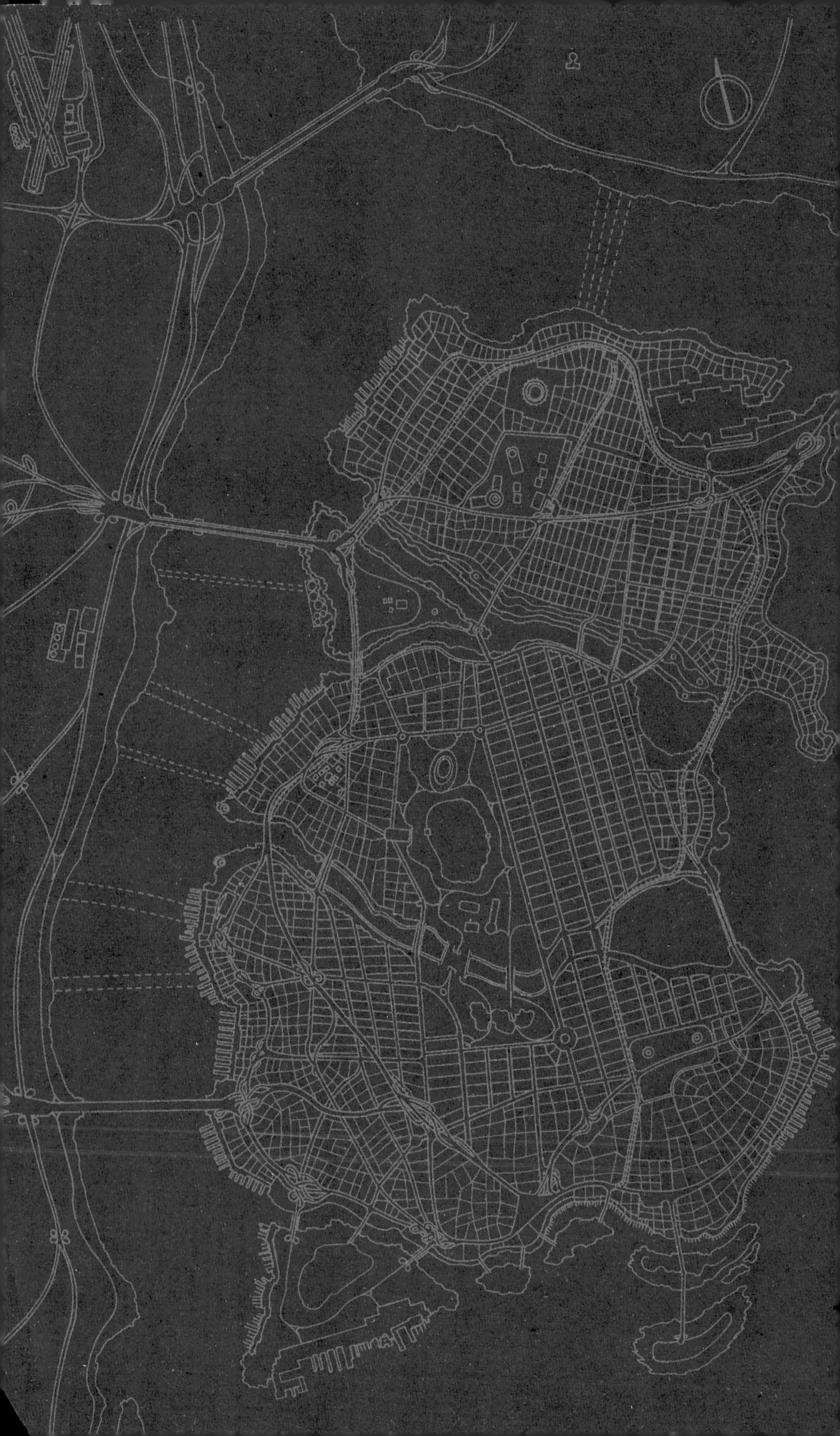

JUNE 23rd -- 6:02 a.m. ...

YOU'RE WASTIN' MY *TIME*, MARCUS. I MEAN IT. WHAT'S THE LIKELIHOOD THAT SOME JUNKIE SNITCH IS GONNA GIVE US A *SERIOUS LEAD* ON THE LEWIS THING?

WHAT, ZERO-TO-NONE?

THAT'S RIGHT, ZERO-TO-NONE...

YET, HERE I AM, *AFTER* OUR SHIFT, WHEN I *COULD* BE CRAWLING INTO BED WITH MY WIFE FOR THOSE FEW HOURS WHEN WE'RE BOTH ASLEEP...

HEY, IF YOU *WANT*, I CAN CHECK INTO THIS BY MYSELF.

AND IF THIS TURNS OUT TO BE THE GUYS? *THEN* WHO'S THE SCHMUCK? I CAN SEE THE HEADLINES--

"DETECTIVE DRIVER NABS LEWIS KIDNAPPERS SINGLE-HANDED."

"PARTNER CHARLIE FIELDS ASLEEP IN CAR." NO THANK YOU.

IT'S A *FOURTEEN-YEAR-OLD-GIRL* BEEN GRABBED, CHARLIE... SURE IT'S *PROBABLY* NOTHING, BUT WHAT DID THAT SNITCH SAY...? THESE GUYS'VE BEEN HIDING OUT AND ACTING *SUSPICIOUS* IN THIS $#!%#@! FOR A *WEEK*.

THE *TIMING'S* RIGHT, AT LEAST.

TIMING'S RIGHT FOR ME TO GET SOME *SLEEP*, TOO...

THEN WE GOT THAT *CEREMONY* TONIGHT, WHICH'LL PROBABLY BE MANDATORY ATTENDANCE...

YEAH YEAH, CRY ME A RIVER. YOU'LL PROBABLY BE HOME IN *TEN* MINUTES.

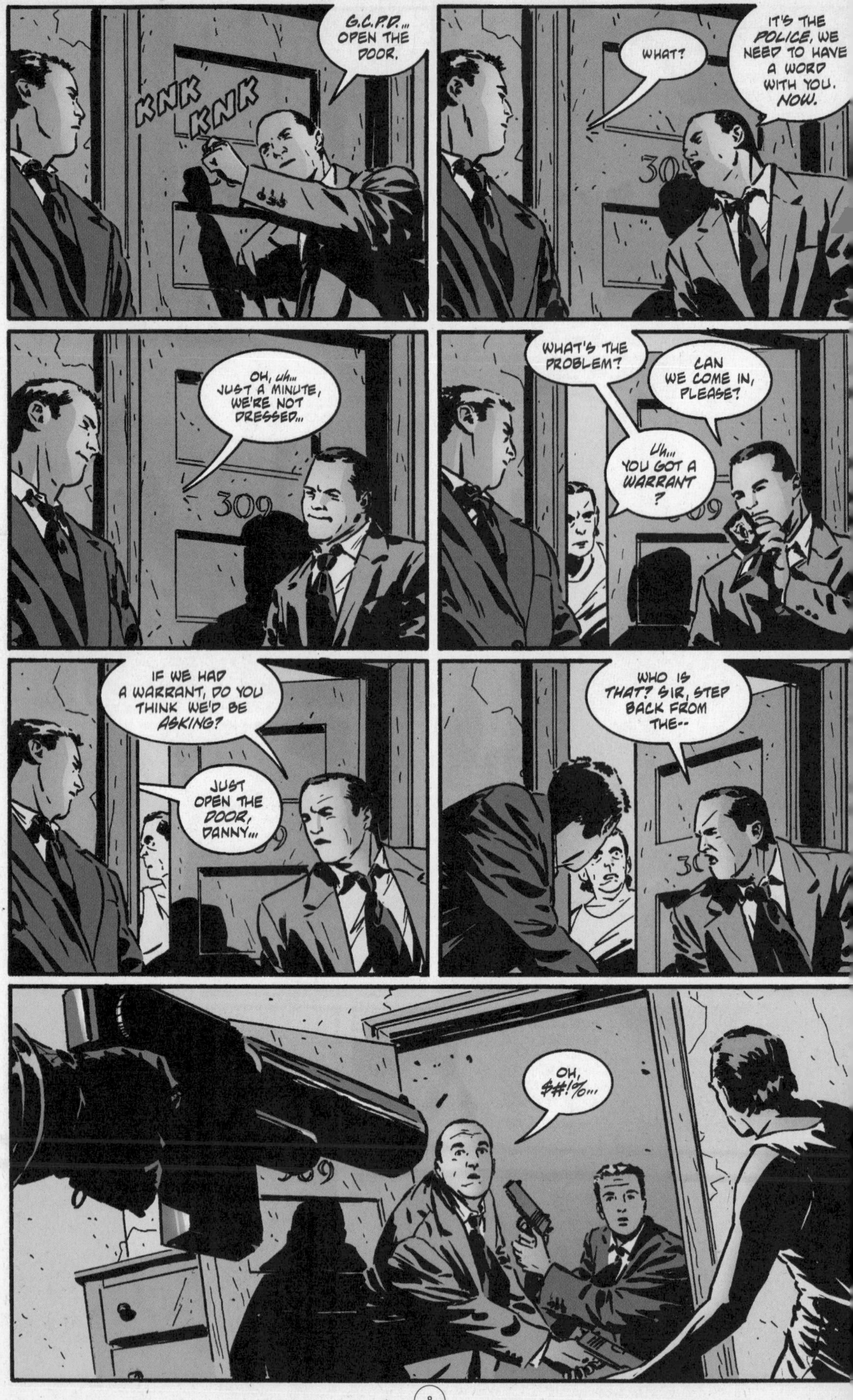
G.C.P.D.... OPEN THE DOOR.
KNK KNK
WHAT?
IT'S THE POLICE, WE NEED TO HAVE A WORD WITH YOU. NOW.
OH, UH... JUST A MINUTE, WE'RE NOT DRESSED...
WHAT'S THE PROBLEM?
CAN WE COME IN, PLEASE?
UH... YOU GOT A WARRANT?
IF WE HAD A WARRANT, DO YOU THINK WE'D BE ASKING?
JUST OPEN THE DOOR, DANNY...
WHO IS THAT? SIR, STEP BACK FROM THE--
OH, $#!%...

IN THE LINE OF DUTY, 1

written by ED BRUBAKER & GREG RUCKA
drawn by MICHAEL LARK

lettered by Willie Schubert
colored by Noelle Giddings
separated by Digital Chameleon
assistant edited by Nachie Castro
edited by Matt Idelson

CHARLIE...?

YOU OKAY?

NO... I'M AFRAID "OKAY" ISN'T A WORD CHARLIE WILL BE USING ANY LONGER...

NOW THEN...

AAAAH!

OH *PLEASE*... STOP. YOUR PARTNER DIDN'T COMPLAIN AT ALL...

NOW, HOW DID YOU *FIND* ME?

THE *HELL* WITH YOU, YOU %@&#$% *PSYCHO*...

YOU KNOW, I'VE *ALWAYS* FOUND THE GOTHAM POLICE TO BE AN INCREDIBLY *UNEDUCATED* LOT...

LET ME GIVE YOU A *LESSON*, DETECTIVE.

chrrk... krrk

SHALL I *CONTINUE*, OR DO YOU WANT TO ANSWER MY *QUESTION*?

WEREN'T AFTER YOU...

WHAT? THE HELL YOU SAY?

TRUE...W-WE HAD A *TIP*, LOOKING FOR KIDNAPPERS...

"THINK WE'D WALK INTO A ROOM WITH...Y-YOU IN IT...WITH NO B-BACKUP?

WELL, IT APPEARS YOU HAD SOME *BAD LUCK* THIS MORNING THEN, DIDN'T YOU?

OF COURSE, I KNOW ABOUT BAD LUCK...THAT'S ONE OF THE LESSONS THAT GOTHAM TEACHES US ALL, EVENTUALLY.

HEY, UH, DON'T YOU THINK WE'D BETTER GET *OUTTA HERE*, FREEZE? SOMEONE MUSTA CALLED IN THAT GUNFIRE.

PLACE'LL BE SWARMIN' WITH *COPS* SOON...

IN A *MINUTE*, DANNY...

...I JUST WANT TO INSTRUCT OUR FRIEND HERE IN GOTHAM'S MORE *ADVANCED CURRICULUM*...THE *TRAGEDY OF SURVIVING LOSS*...

...AS A *PREVIEW* OF *THINGS TO COME*.

MORNING, STACY.

MORNING, DETECTIVE. HAVE A GOOD REST.

HEY, COHEN!

SECOND SHIFT GET ANY OF THOSE DOUGHNUTS?

HELL, NO, CROWE.

GOTHAM DONUTS

WE DONE?

YEAH, WE'RE FINISHED...

--THINK THE POLITICAL SITUATION IN THIS CITY IS GOING TO *CHANGE*, RENEE, THEN YOU'RE *NOT* PAYING *ATTENTION.*

ALL I ASKED WAS IF YOU WERE GOING *TONIGHT*, CHRIS, THAT'S *ALL...*

...WENT LAST NIGHT?

PRETTY *QUIET*, MUST BE THE *HEAT*. GONNA BE A *LONG* SUMMER.

HEY! WHICH ONE OF YOU LEFT YOUR *DINNER* ON MY *DESK?*

MARGARET SAWYER

CAPTAIN SAYWER.

LIEUTENANT PROBSON.

THOUGHT YOU'D HAVE GONE ALREADY.

FINISHING UP O.T.S.

ANYTHING I SHOULD KNOW?

NAH, IT WAS *DEAD* LAST NIGHT. ALL *MY* KIDS ARE ACCOUNTED FOR.

FIELDS AND DRIVER ARE STILL *OUT.* FOLLOWING UP ON A TIP BEFORE THEY GO OFF-SHIFT.

THAT THE *LEWIS* THING?

YEAH. STILL *NOTHING.* THEY'RE GRASPING AT *STRAWS.*

YOU WANT ANY OF *MINE* TO LOOK INTO IT?

PROCJNOW AND BURKE ARE *CLEAR*--

IT'S *COVERED* CAPTAIN. WE'VE GOT IT. WE DON'T NEED *YOUR* HELP.

IT BOTHERS YOU *THAT* MUCH? THAT I GOT THE *PROMOTION?*

OR MAYBE IT'S *SOMETHING ELSE* THAT'S EATING YOU, *LIEUTENANT?*

YOU'RE NOT *CATCHING ME* IN SOME *HARASSMENT* THING--

CAPTAIN!

MRGARET AWYER

H COMMANDER

JUST CAME *IN,* OFFICER *DOWN*--

--IT'S DETECTIVES DRIVER AND *FIELDS,* CAPTAIN...

DETECTIVE DRIVER...?

...I'M SORRY... DETECTIVE...

WE'RE GONNA TRY AND *MOVE* YOU NOW...

OH, UH... YEAH, SURE, OKAY...

IS *THIS* OKAY? CAN YOU MOVE YOUR ARMS?

YEAH, JUST NOT MY *HANDS*...

THEY'VE GOT A CREW DOWNSTAIRS THAT'LL TAKE CARE OF THAT FOR YOU, SIR... YOU'RE GOING TO BE *FINE*.

MAN... HOW THE &@$% ARE THEY GONNA GET THIS GUY TO THE MORGUE? IN A COUPLE OF *FREEZER BAGS?*

SHUT UP, TODD... OKAY?

WHAT, WHAT'D I SAY?

DRIVER! *THERE YOU ARE...* WHERE'S *CHARLIE?* WHAT THE HOLY HELL IS *GOING ON* HERE?

DID HE--

--OH, *GOD...* YOUR *HANDS.* WHAT HAPPENED TO YOUR HANDS?

CHARLIE'S *DEAD,* LIEUTENANT...

CHARLIE... DAMN...

WELL--WHAT ARE YOU *STANDING HERE* FOR? GET THIS MAN SOME MEDICAL ATTENTION AND THEN GET HIM BACK TO CENTRAL...

I WAS ON MY *WAY,* SIR.

HANG IN THERE, DRIVER... JUST HANG IN THERE.

SORRY ABOUT THAT.

HE'S *MY* BOSS, NOT YOURS...

WELL, STILL....

HOW COME YOU ALWAYS GIVE ME THE JUICY ONES, CAPTAIN?

BECAUSE YOU'RE MY FAVORITE, CRIS.

EXCEPT THIS TIME, YOU'RE NOT.

THIS ONE'S YOURS, RENEE...

...PUT IT DOWN.

I'LL CALL IN BOTH SHIFTS, THEY'LL BE AT YOUR DISPOSAL.

MARCUS.

I'M SORRY.

YEAH. IT WAS *FREEZE*.

I *HEARD.*

WE'LL TALK WHEN I GET BACK TO THE *SQUADROOM,* OKAY?

I'LL TAKE YOUR *STATEMENT* THEN.

SURE.

...KNOW ABOUT FREEZE?

JUST WHAT I'VE READ.

HAS A SUIT. NEEDS IT TO LIVE. CAN'T STAND HEAT.

A LITTLE SIMPLE, BUT YEAH...

...MOTHER OF GOD...

PARTNER?

RENEE?

THEY DO STANDARD ENTRY, RIGHT?

WHAT?

PROBSON SAID THAT FIELDS AND DRIVER WERE JUST CHECKING OUT A *TIP* ON THE LEWIS KIDNAPPING.

AND THEY'RE FIGURING IT'S A *BOGUS* TIP TOO, BECAUSE THEY DON'T EVEN HAVE A *BACK-UP.*

RIGHT, THEY'RE NOT *EXPECTING* ANY KIND OF REAL TROUBLE.

SO THEY KNOCK ON THE DOOR AND *FREEZE* JUST GOES *BOOM.*

WHY?

WHY DOESN'T HE JUST *HOOF* IT WHEN THEY *DECLARE...*

JUST GO OUT THE *WINDOW* HERE?

McCALL'S FURNAS AND FR

"...HE WANTS TO KNOW HOW THEY *FOUND* HIM?

FREEZE DOESN'T *CARE* ABOUT THAT, C'MON..."

"...HE COULD'VE KILLED THEM *BOTH*, WE'D NEVER HAVE *KNOWN* UNTIL DRIVER AND FIELDS DIDN'T SHOW UP TONIGHT.

BUT FREEZE LEAVES MARCUS *ALIVE.*

WHY?

Charlie Fields

river

MARCUS...?

HEY, SARGE... YOU ALL GET CALLED IN?

YEAH, I'M JUST THE FIRST TO ARRIVE, KID... GUESS NONE OF US'RE SLEEPIN' *TODAY*...

YOU WANNA TELL ME WHAT WENT DOWN?

NOT MUCH TO TELL. KNOCKED ON THE WRONG DOOR...

YOU KNOW WHAT THIS *MEANS*, RIGHT?

22

YEAH, I KNOW...

DAMN... YOU KNOW WHAT'S FUNNY?

FUNNY?

NO, WHAT?

WHEN CHARLIE FIRST CAME OVER TO THE M.C.U., HE THOUGHT IT'D BE A REAL BIG JOKE TO PUT *THE BAT* UP ON THE BOARD, LIKE HE WAS PART OF THE SQUAD, TOO.

HE WAS TRYIN' TO SHAME US ALL BY SHOWIN' HOW MUCH HIGHER THAT FREAK'S CLEARANCE RATE WAS THAN OURS.

THING IS, WE LEFT HIS NAME UP THERE, AND WHENEVER THE JOKER OR TWO-FACE OR *WHOEVER* KILLED SOMEBODY, AND WE COULDN'T CLOSE IT...

...WE'D PUT THE VIC'S NAME UNDER THE BAT'S, LIKE IT WAS *HIS* CASE NOW.

THEN *THE PROBE* TOOK OVER 2nd SHIFT AND MADE US ERASE IT... SAID IT WAS *DEMORALIZING* TO THE SQUAD.

AND CHARLIE, HE SAYS, "WELL, THAT'S THE *POINT*, LIEUTEN-ANT."

HE *WANTED* THAT CONSTANT REMINDER THAT IF *WE* DIDN'T DO OUR JOB, SOME-ONE ELSE *WOULD*...

...CHARLIE WAS JUST FUNNY THAT WAY.

--IT'S STILL TOO EARLY TO SAY, FOR SURE, BUT I DO *PLAN* ON ATTENDING... YES.

NO, THEY'RE AT THE *SCENE*... I IMAGINE THEY'LL GIVE ME A PRELIMINARY RUN-DOWN SOON, THOUGH...

MISTER *MAYOR?* I'VE GOT TO GO... I'LL REPORT IN AS SOON AS I HAVE ANYTHING.

HAVE A SEAT, DETECTIVE DRIVER...

IF IT'S ALL RIGHT WITH YOU I'LL *STAND,* SIR...

I KNOW I DON'T HAVE TO TELL YOU HOW SORRY I AM ABOUT YOUR *PARTNER*... BUT I *AM* SORRY. CHARLIE FIELDS WAS A GOOD COP.

TOO BAD HE WASN'T A REAL PIECE OF #$#%@! THOUGH, ISN'T IT?

THEN I WOULDN'T FEEL SO BAD THAT HE DIED SAVING ME...

YOU'D FEEL BAD JUST THE SAME.

WAS THERE SOMETHING YOU WANTED TO SEE ME ABOUT?

I WANT TO ASK YOU NOT TO USE THE *SIGNAL*... TO LET US HANDLE THIS ONE BY OURSELVES.

EXCUSE ME?

24

WE *NEED* TO BRING THIS FREAK DOWN ON *OUR OWN.* HE TOOK CHARLIE AND MADE HIM INTO *ICE CUBES,* COMMISSIONER, AND WE NEED TO TAKE HIM DOWN WITHOUT HELP...

...FOR CHARLIE'S SAKE IF NOT FOR OURS...

I *AGREE* WITH YOU... BUT MISTER FREEZE IS IN GOTHAM, WHICH MEANS THERE'S *MORE* AT STAKE HERE THAN OUR *PRIDE,* DETECTIVE.

BESIDES, DO YOU *REALLY* THINK I COULD STOP BATMAN JUST BY NOT ASKING HIM TO HELP?

I DON'T *KNOW...* PROBABLY NOT. BUT MAYBE YOU COULD MAKE HIM UNDERSTAND WHAT IT *MEANS* TO US TO HAVE TO TURN ON THAT *DAMN* SIGNAL.

ALL I KNOW IS, WE *CAN'T* TURN IT ON TODAY... WE *CAN'T...*

YOU'VE GOT A ROOM FILLING UP WITH COPS OUT THERE... KNOWING IF THEY DON'T GET THIS GUY BY *DARK...* THEN... I MEAN...

...IT'S JUST NOT FAIR, SIR...

IF IT MAKES YOU FEEL ANY BETTER, I DON'T PLAN TO CALL FOR HIM UNLESS I ABSOLUTELY *HAVE TO.* I WANT US TO DO THIS AS MUCH AS YOU DO.

KN'K KN'K

SORRY TO DISTURB YOU, COMMISSIONER... BUT DETECTIVES *ALLEN* AND *MONTOYA* ARE BACK, AND THEY NEED TO TALK TO DETECTIVE *DRIVER...*

OKAY, STACY. TELL THEM HE'LL BE RIGHT THERE...

WE'LL CONTINUE THIS CONVERSATION LATER, DETECTIVE. YOU GO DO YOUR JOB NOW, OKAY?

LET *ME* WORRY ABOUT THE REST...

YES, SIR, THANK YOU...

YOU UP TO THIS, MARCUS? YOU WANT ANYTHING BEFORE WE START?

NO, LET'S JUST GET ON WITH IT...

...I HAVE TO MEET NORA AT THE *MORGUE* IN A COUPLE MINUTES.

WON'T TAKE US LONG.

YOU WANT ME TO TELL IT?

I THINK WE'VE GOT MOST OF IT.

IS IT *POSSIBLE*, THIS INFORMANT OF YOURS, HE WAS SETTING YOU TWO UP?

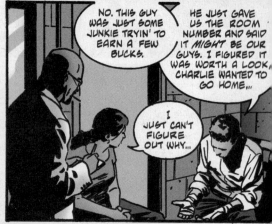

NO. THIS GUY WAS JUST SOME JUNKIE TRYIN' TO EARN A FEW BUCKS.

HE JUST GAVE US THE ROOM NUMBER AND SAID IT *MIGHT* BE OUR GUYS. I FIGURED IT WAS WORTH A LOOK, CHARLIE WANTED TO GO HOME...

I JUST CAN'T FIGURE OUT WHY...

...WHY HE LEFT YOU *ALIVE*, MARCUS.

HE HAD TO *KNOW* WE'D PULL OUT ALL THE STOPS TO FIND HIM.

INCLUDING THE *BAT*.

MAYBE HE'S TRYING TO GET BATMAN'S ATTENTION.

MAYBE, BUT AGAIN, *WHY*?

COULD WE LEAVE THE BAT OUT OF THIS FOR NOW?

YOU THINK? MAYBE?

SURE, DETECTIVE.

I UNDERSTAND.

I DON'T *KNOW* WHY HE'S *CRAZY*, RENEE. YOU'VE READ THE *FILE.*

FREEZE WANTS PEOPLE TO *HURT.* NOT *PHYSICALLY.* EMOTIONALLY.

TAKE TWO COPS, KILL A *PARTNER...*

...INSTANT *GRIEF.*

"...SEE...IT DOESN'T *FIT* THE PROFILE.

JOKER, I'D *BELIEVE* THAT.

BUT *FREEZE* IS SMARTER THAN HE IS *CRAZY.*

SO, HE'S GOTTA BE SENDING SOME KIND OF *MESSAGE* IF HE LET YOU *LIVE...*

TRYING TO LET US KNOW HE'S *SMARTER* THAN US.

IF YOU *SAY* SO...PERSONALLY--

GUYS, WE GOT A CALL COMING IN YOU *MIGHT* WANNA TAKE...

SERGEANT, WE'RE IN THE MIDDLE OF--

JUST *TRUST* ME, OKAY?

WHAT IS IT?

UNIFORM JUST CALLED IN, HE'S ON LINE TWO, SOUNDS PRETTY *SHOOK UP*...

...LONG AND SHORT OF IT, THOUGH, IS WE GOT ANOTHER *FROZEN* BODY.

THIS IS DETECTIVE *MONTOYA*, WHO AM I SPEAKING TO?

ALL RIGHT, OFFICER DUMFY... WE'VE GOT PEOPLE ON THE WAY *RIGHT NOW*, DON' WORRY...

OKAY, DETECTIVE... BUT TELL THEM TO *HURRY.* IT LOOKS LIKE SOMEBODY FROZE THIS GUY FROM THE *INSIDE OUT*...

...AND NO OFFENSE, MA'AM... BUT I *DON'T* WANT TO BE STANDIN' HERE IF HE DECIDES TO COME *BACK*...

JUNE 23rd -- 1:37 P.M. ...

ANY IDEA *HOW LONG* HE'S BEEN LIKE THIS?

NAH, WE'RE *NOT* GETTING *ANYTHING* USEFUL FROM A GUY WHO'S BEEN FROZEN FROM THE INSIDE OUT LIKE THIS...

HAVE TO GET TIME OF DEATH ON THIS ONE FROM *WITNESSES*--

--OR MAYBE WE'LL GET *LUCKY* WITH SOMETHING IN THE CAR...

HEY, CAREFUL NOT TO *BREAK* HIM....

LIKE WE'VE GOT A *CHOICE...*

Krak

OH, MAN...

I KNOW...

SO, WHAT DO YOU THINK?

SAME AS *YOU*--

FREEZE PUT HIS GUN RIGHT IN THAT POOR #@$%'S MOUTH, TURNED IT ON FULL BLAST...

PROBABLY HURT LIKE HELL.

YOU THINK?

SO, MARCUS, YOU'RE *ABSOLUTELY* SURE THAT WAS THE GUY WHO WAS WORKIN' WITH *FREEZE?*

YEAH, EXCEPT FOR THE BULGING EYES AND BLUE LIPS, HE'S THE *SPITTING IMAGE.*

WELL, THAT'S NOT GOOD AT ALL, THEN, IS IT?

OBVIOUSLY, WHATEVER HE NEEDED *BACKUP* FOR HAS BEEN DONE.

AND I DON'T LIKE THE LOOKS OF THAT TRUCK EITHER... THEY WERE HAULING SOMETHING SOMEWHERE...

GOD, THIS DAY JUST GETS *BETTER,* DOESN'T IT?

YEAH, I'M AFRAID IT *DOES...*

HANG ON... I'LL RIDE WITH YOU...

WHAT, YOU HEADED TO THE MORGUE?

YEAH, I AM...

IN THE LINE OF DUTY 2

written by ED BRUBAKER & GREG RUCKA
drawn by MICHAEL LARK

lettered by Willie Schubert
colored by Noelle Giddings
separated by Digital Chameleon
assistant edited by Nachie Castro
edited by Matt Idelson

LISTEN... ARE YOU SURE YOU'RE UP TO THIS, NORA?

I WORK IN THIS MORGUE, MARCUS, AND MY HUSBAND IS--WAS-- A COP...

KANE COUNTY MORGUE

I DON'T HAVE ANY ILLUSIONS ABOUT LIFE AND DEATH.

I KNOW, BUT... THIS IS DIFFERENT... HE'S NOT... UH--

I KNOW THAT, TOO. CAPTAIN SAWYER TOLD ME...

BECAUSE YOU DON'T HAVE TO IDENTIFY HIM, OFFICIALLY, WE KNOW WHO HE IS... AND I REALLY DON'T THINK YOU--

--LOOK, I HAVE TO SEE HIM... IT'S NOT GOING TO BE REAL UNTIL I SEE HIM, OKAY?

I LOOK AT DEAD PEOPLE ALL DAY LONG AND EVERY NIGHT I WAIT FOR THE PHONE TO RING OR SOMEONE TO KNOCK ON THE DOOR... TO TELL ME...

AND-- AND... IT JUST DOESN'T FEEL REAL SOMEHOW...

IT'S OKAY, NORA...

SO I DON'T CARE WHAT THEY DID TO HIM, OKAY?...

I HAVE TO SEE...

NOTIC

Oh, uh... NORA... I, uh... I'M--

IT'S ALL RIGHT, BILL, YOU DON'T HAVE TO SAY ANYTHING...

YES, WELL... WE, UH, WE HAD TO PUT HIM IN *HERE*... I'M SORRY, BUT...

...IT'S JUST, WE *TRIED* TO THAW HIM OUT, BUT HE STARTED... *MELTING*...

WE DON'T COMPLETELY UNDERSTAND HOW, BUT HIS ENTIRE CELLULAR STRUCTURE HAS BEEN TURNED TO ICE... IT'S *IRREVERSIBLE.*

HE'S NOT... HE'S NOT A *PRETTY SIGHT* I'M AFRAID, NORA...

OH, GOD... CHARLIE...

WHAT DID THEY *DO* TO MY CHARLIE?

WHAT DID THEY DO, MARCUS? HOW COULD SOMEONE...?

I'M SO SORRY... I COULDN'T SAVE HIM...

...I'M SORRY...

...LISTEN UP, PEOPLE!

DETECTIVE MONTOYA?

THANKS, CAPTAIN.

OKAY... TO MAKE SURE EVERYONE'S ON THE SAME PAGE I'M GOING TO HIT THESE POINTS AGAIN IN BRIEF.

AT APPROX OH-SIX THIS MORNING DETECTIVES FIELDS AND DRIVER WENT TO QUESTION SOME MEN AT THE WHARFSIDE INN ON A TIP IN CONNECTION WITH THE LEWIS KIDNAPPING.

FREEZE

AT THE HOTEL THEY ENCOUNTERED VICTOR FRIES WITH AN UNIDENTIFIED ASSOCIATE KNOWN ONLY AS "DANNY."

FRIES SUBDUED BOTH DETECTIVES, THEN MURDERED DETECTIVE FIELDS. SOMETIME IN THE NEXT FEW HOURS HE ALSO APPARENTLY KILLED DANNY...

AND NOW YOU KNOW EVERYTHING WE DO.

DETECTIVE AZEVEDA?

ANY CHANCE FREEZE IS CONNECTED TO THE LEWIS GRAB?

NO...

...IT WAS JUST ROTTEN %$&^ING LUCK, JOSH.

THE LEWIS KIDNAPPING HAS BEEN HANDED TO THE F.B.I. FOR THE TIME BEING...

...DETECTIVE FIELDS' MURDER IS OUR ONLY PRIORITY RIGHT NOW.

THERE ARE A COUPLE OF THINGS WE *KNOW* FOR CERTAIN ABOUT *FREEZE.*

HE CAN'T *LIVE* WITHOUT HIS SUIT, AND APPARENTLY THE SUIT REQUIRES *DIAMONDS* TO FUNCTION...

FREEZE
- ORGANIZED CRIMINAL
- INTELLIGENT
- DEPENDS ON SUIT
- DIAMONDS
- TECHNICAL SAVVY

...AND HE STRIKES AT THE *HEART* OF HIS VICTIMS.

FREEZE
- ORGANIZED CRIMINA
- INTELLIGENT
- EPENDS ON SUIT
- DIAMONDS
- ECHNICAL SAVVY
- DES FOR
- EMOTIONAL RE

FREEZE
- ORGANIZED CRIMINA
- INTELLIGENT
- DE ON SUIT
- SAVVY
- RESPO

HE LIKES PEOPLE TO *SUFFER.*

FREEZE
- ORGANIZED CRIMI
- GENT
- ON SUIT
- RS
- L SAVVY
- L RESP

WE DON'T KNOW *WHAT* HE'S PLANNING OR *WHERE.*

PROBABLY SOMETHING *BIG*-- DANNY'S CORPSE WAS FOUND WITH AN EMPTY TRUCK--LOOKS LIKE THEY WERE *HAULING* SOMETHING--

--AND IT'S GOT TO BE *SOON,* BECAUSE *FREEZE* KNOWS AS WELL AS *WE* DO, AS SOON AS THE SUN GOES DOWN...HE'S GOING TO HAVE A *BAT* UP HIS $%#.

OKAY, CHRIS HAS THE *ASSIGN-MENTS...*

FREEZE? YOU'RE KIDDING ME, RIGHT!

YEAH, HE'S REAL BIG ON KEEPIN' IN TOUCH, AIN'T HE?

THINK I JUST GOT A POSTCARD FROM HIM THE OTHER DAY...

RIGHT...

I DUNNO NUTHIN', MAN...

BUT IF HE'S PLANNIN' SOMETHING BIG, YOU MIGHT WANNA STAY OUTTA HIS WAY...

'CAUSE, LIKE I SAID, I AIN'T IN ON ANY OF HIS ACTION ANYMORE...

...BUT THAT MOTHER IS NOT TO BE MESSED WITH...

WELL... THAT WAS PRODUCTIVE. HOW DID WE END UP WITH THE KNOWN-ASSOCIATE DETAIL?

I GUESS ALLEN MUST'VE HEARD HOW THE SMELL OF HOLDING CELLS BRINGS BACK MEMORIES OF THOSE BOARDING SCHOOL DAYS FOR YOU, TREY...

YES, THAT MUST'VE BEEN IT...

...THOUGH I CAN'T HELP BUT THINK MY EXPERIENCE WOULD'VE COME IN A LITTLE MORE HANDY QUESTIONING THE CITY'S DIAMOND MERCHANTS.

WHAT, YOU DON'T THINK SARGE HAS A LIGHT ENOUGH TOUCH FOR THOSE POWDERPUFFS?

WHAT I'M TELLING YOU IS I HAVE A DEAD COP--

--AND THE GUY WHO KILLED HIM NEEDS DIAMONDS JUST TO BREATHE!

SO, I DON'T CARE ABOUT YOUR TAXES OR YOUR INSURANCE, I JUST WANT YOU TO ANSWER THE QUESTION.

NO, I DON'T KNOW OF ANY DIAMOND THEFTS OF ANY REAL CONCERN IN THE PAST FEW MONTHS... I CERTAINLY HAVEN'T HAD ANY GO MISSING.

OKAY, WELL, WHAT ABOUT ANY *OFF-THE-BOOKS* DEALS?

YOU HEAR ABOUT ANY *BLACK MARKET* STONES THAT'VE GONE MISSING LATELY?

BLACK MARKET?

I'M NOT SURE I UNDERSTAND YOUR *IMPLICATION*, OFFICER...

WHAT BLACK MARKET ARE YOU TALKING ABOUT?

CROWE, I SWEAR TO GOD I'M GONNA *DECK* THIS @$$#%!#...

BAD MOVE SWINGING ON MY PARTNER THERE, RICO.

DIDN'T YOU KNOW ROMY HAD THE *BLACK BELT*?

DAMN, THINK I BROKE MY *HAND*, NATE...

NOW ARE YOU GONNA TELL US ABOUT THOSE *DIAMONDS*, OR NOT?

ALL I KNOW IS WHAT I *HEARD*, HOLMES... SOMEONE JUST JACKED A BUNCH OF STONES FROM THE *ODESSA MOB*, MAN, AND THE RUSSIANS'RE %!$$@# ABOUT IT, MAN...

WHAT KIND OF WEIGHT ARE WE TALKING ABOUT?

WHAT I HEARD *HEAVY* WEIGHT...

LOOKIN' AT *TWENTY MIL*...

HAD SOME FOREIGN BUYER ALL LINED UP OR SOMETHIN'...

WE BETTER CALL DAVIES...

TWENTY MILLION IN DIAMONDS COULD DO A *LOT* OF DAMAGE IN MISTER FREEZE'S HANDS...

"...WELL, TO KEEP ICE FOR A START.

LIKE IN ORGAN TRANSPLANTS?

HEARTFELT MEDICAL SUPPLIES

WELL, WE DON'T HANDLE STUFF LIKE THAT HERE.

WE SUPPLY SOME STUFF TO HOSPITALS, BUT NOTHING LIKE THAT.

THANKS FOR YOUR TIME--

YOU KNOW SOMETHING? I JUST THOUGHT OF SOMETHING...

THERE'S A PLACE JUST OPENED, KINDA A QUACK THING. CALLED...UH, WHAT IS IT...

"...SOMETHING CRYOGENICS... LIKE CHATTER OR UH FROSTY OR...

"...ANY PROBLEMS WITH MATERIAL GOING MISSING OR ANYTHING LIKE THAT?

shiver

"...I'M SORRY, WHAT WAS THAT, DETECTIVE?

DETECTIVE PROCJNOW WAS ASKING IF YOU'RE MISSING ANYTHING.

OH, NO. NOTHING LIKE THAT, AT LEAST.

WELL, MAYBE WE COULD SEE YOUR INVENTORY LISTS?

IF YOU'RE NOT TOO BUSY...

OH, SURE, HERE THEY ARE.

I COULD HELP YOU GO THROUGH THEM, IF YOU LIKE...

MOVE A *LOT* OF THESE, DO YOU?

NICK'S RESTAURANT SUPPLY

THESE? NAW, WE'VE ONLY EVER SOLD *TWO* OF THEM.

REALLY? WHO BOUGHT THEM?

YEAH, SEE, I *REMEMBER* THEM *BOTH* 'CUZ IT'S SO RARE THAT WE SELL THEM AT ALL.

WE SOLD ONE TO WAYNE, YOU KNOW, BEFORE HE WENT *CRAZY...* RIGHT AFTER N.M.L...

...AND THE OTHER TO THE *GOVERNMENT* FOR THE NATIONAL GUARD BARRACKS.

AH, WELL... THANKS FOR YOUR HELP.

...NOT SAYING IT'LL BE ANYTHING BUT IT'S BETTER THAN DOING *NOTHING.*

YOU AND I *BOTH* KNOW THIS IS GOING TO END UP IN THE BAT'S *HANDS,* RENEE.

I UNDERSTAND DRIVER'S CONCERN, BUT WE'RE NOT TALKING ABOUT SOME *STREET SKEL* HERE.

MAYBE IT'S TIME TO USE A *BIG GUN,* YOU KNOW?

I REMEMBER WHEN YOU FIRST SHOWED UP HERE, YOU WERE NOT *DOWN* WITH BATMAN AT ALL.

TIMES *CHANGE.*

ANYTHING?

NOTHING.

LET'S HEAD BACK...

...PRACTICALLY *BLOWING* IN MY *PARTNER'S EAR,* THERE.

LEAVING *ME* TO DO THE *DETECTIVE WORK,* I MIGHT ADD.

HE GET A PHONE *NUMBER?*

YOU THINK HE'S GONNA *SHARE* WITH *YOU,* DETECTIVE PATTON?

I THOUGHT YOU HAD A THING FOR CHANDLER, ANYWAY--

HEY, LISTEN, PROCJ/NOW--

ALL RIGHT, LET'S *HEAR* IT...

...WHAT DO YOU *GOT?* DETECTIVE HARTLEY?

NOTHING FROM THE *KNOWN* ASSOCIATES.

THEY DON'T SPEAK *HIGHLY* OF FREEZE AS AN *EMPLOYER.*

SURPRISING, WE *KNOW.*

NO REPORTED *THEFTS* FROM THE *LEGIT* BUSINESSES AT LEAST.

BUT ROMY AND NATE GOT SOMETHING *INTERESTING...*

"...YEAH, SOMEONE HIT THE ODESSA BOYS FOR 20 MIL IN ICE.

THAT'S WORD ON THE STREET, THOUGH, SO TAKE IT FOR WHAT IT'S WORTH.

WELL, WHATEVER FREEZE USES, IT'S CUSTOM.

MEDICAL SUPPLY DOESN'T HAVE ANYTHING EVEN CLOSE.

TWENTY MIL IN DIAMONDS.

HOW MANY DOES THIS GUY NEED TO MAKE HIS GIZMOS GO?

WELL, INTERESTING THAT YOU WOULD ASK THAT, RENEE...

...AS MY PARTNER GOT A CRASH COURSE IN THE ART AND SCIENCE OF THE DEEP FREEZE.

WAY IT WORKS, DOESN'T ACTUALLY TAKE SO MUCH ENERGY TO FREEZE SOMETHING.

KEEPING IT FROZE, THAT'S THE TRICK.

SO SOMETHING BIG.

BUT WE DON'T KNOW WHERE. WE DON'T KNOW WHEN.

ALLEN AND I CHECKED THE PLACE BY THE INN...

...IT'S AN ABANDONED HEATING PLACE. USED TO SELL FURNACES AND OIL HEATERS.

AND AIR CONDITIONERS.

GOD, IT'S HOT IN HERE...

OKAY, LET'S GO OVER IT AGAIN...

LESSON ONE!

YOU KNOW... GOTHAM POLICE... INCREDIBLY UNEDUCATED LOT...

...INSTRUCT OUR FRIEND... GOTHAM'S MORE ADVANCED CURRICULUM...

THE PRESIDENT, FACULTY AND GRADUATES
of Gotham University...

CONFE...
HONORARY...
IN THE FIEL...
TO MR. F...

COMMENCEMENT...
FRIDAY, JUNE TWENY-THIRD...
GOTHAM UNIVERSITY, MI...

FREEZE

DAMN IT! THAT SON OF A--

MARCUS?

IT'S BEEN RIGHT IN FRONT OF US ALL *DAMN* DAY...

THE SICK #$@!%# PRACTICALLY GAVE US A HAND-WRITTEN INVITATION...

...EXCEPT WE ALREADY GOT THE *PRINTED* VERSION A WEEK AGO.

OH MY GOD...

IT'S LIKE THE WHOLE DAY IS JUST *ONE BIG JOKE...* ISN'T IT?

COMMISSIONER, WE *HAVE* TO TURN ON THE *SIGNAL,* RIGHT NOW!

WHAT? I THOUGHT YOU--

THERE'RE TOO MANY LIVES INVOLVED NOW, SIR...

IT'S TOO BIG FOR US.

"...UNDERCOVER! REMEMBER!

WE DON'T WANT TO START A PANIC!

USE YOUR EARPIECES. STAY ON THE NET.

BUT NOBODY MOVE UNTIL WE'VE GOT Q.R.T. IN PLACE!

YOU SUPERVISE THE FLOOR UNTIL I GET THERE.

I'LL TALK TO HENELLY, FOLLOW THEM OUT.

GOT IT.

LIEUTENANT HENELLY?

CAPTAIN SAWYER IN THE M.C.U....

"...GET Q.R.T. MOBILIZED AND DOWN TO G.S.U.--

THAT'S RIGHT, WE THINK FREEZE IS GOING FOR THE CEREMONY...

THE PRESIDENT, FACULTY AND GRADUATING CLASS OF GOTHAM STATE UNIVERSITY ANNOUNCE THE

CONFERRING OF THE HONORARY DEGREE OF DOCT IN THE FIELD OF CRI TO MR. F

COMMENC FRIDAY, JUNE 7 VERY GOTHAM STATE UNIV

Miss Sau c/o G.C.P. Major C

PICK UP DRESS FROM CLEANERS

IF YOU DON'T MIND, COMMISSIONER, I'D LIKE TO DO IT MYSELF...

I'M AFRAID I CAN'T ALLOW THAT...

THE G.C.P.D. CAN'T OFFICIALLY TOUCH THE BAT-SIGNAL, OR IN ANY WAY ACKNOWLEDGE THE EXISTENCE OF BATMAN.

SO WE'RE CALLING HIM IN TO TAKE DOWN MISTER FREEZE, BUT WE CAN'T ADMIT HE'S REAL?

IT'S A FINE LINE, I KNOW.

GO AHEAD, STACY...

SO YOU'RE OKAY WITH THIS THEN?

NO... BUT I'M A COP IN GOTHAM. I CAN'T AFFORD TO LIVE IN DENIAL...

I'VE NEVER ACTUALLY BEEN HERE FOR THIS...

HOW LONG DOES IT USUALLY TAKE FOR HIM TO SHOW?

WITH HIM, IT'S ALWAYS SOONER THAN YOU THINK...

TALK.

44

...IN POSITION OUTSIDE, WHERE ELSE?

WELL, HE'S NOT GOING TO BE IN THE CROWD.

YOU THINK HE'S JUST GOING AFTER *HIM?*

MAYBE HE WANTS TO GET THE WHOLE DAMN *ROOM?*

MILLER AUDITORIUM
Gotham State University

THAT'S A COMFORTING THOUGHT...

...KEEP ME *WARM* AT NIGHT.

THAT'S *VERY FUNNY,* ROMY--

THIS IS HENELLY, EVERYONE SHUT UP.

ROOF ACCESS

THANK YOU.

THIS IS Q.R.T. LEADER. ALL *POSTS,* CONFIRM POSITIONS. GREEN TEAMS?

GREEN ONE, GOOD. SOUTH ENTRANCE SECURE.

GREEN TWO, GOOD. PARKING LOT SECURE.

GREEN THREE, GOOD. BACKSTAGE SECURE.

CONFIRMED. RED TEAMS?

RED ONE, GROUND SECURE.

RED TWO, ROOFTOP SECURE.

EAST STAIRWELL
AUTHORIZED PERSONNEL ONLY

RED THREE, SUBLEVEL SECURE.

CONFIRMED. NO SIGN OF FREEZE...

...WHERE THE HELL IS HE?

THIS IS SAWYER.

THEY'RE STARTING THE CEREMONY.

LADIES AND GENTLEMEN, WELCOME TO THE FORTY-THIRD *COMMENCEMENT* OF GOTHAM STATE UNIVERSITY.

WE WILL BEGIN WITH *REMARKS* FROM THIS YEAR'S *DISTINGUISHED GUEST...*

...A MAN KNOWN TO US ALL AS A DEDICATED PUBLIC SERVANT.

HE IS THIS YEAR'S *RECIPIENT* OF THE J.K. MANNING AWARD FOR SERVICE TO THE COMMUNITY...

"...AND HAS JUST BEEN CONFERRED AN HONORARY DOCTORATE IN THE FIELD OF CRIMINOLOGY..."

"...MAY I PRESENT TO YOU GOTHAM CITY'S FORMER COMMISSIONER OF POLICE..."

JAMES GORDON.

CLAPCLAPCLAPCLAPCLA

ANYTHING?

NOTHING.

NOTHING AT ALL.

CLAPCLAPCLA CLAPCLAPCLA

THANK YOU, THANK YOU VERY MUCH...

IT'S A HELL OF A NICE WAY TO BE WELCOMED HOME, I'LL TELL YOU *THAT*.

I DON'T HAVE *MUCH* TO SAY, I'M AFRAID, SO YOU *KIDS* ARE GETTING OFF *EASY*. I'M GOING TO BE *BRIEF*.

BIG *DAY* FOR YOU. GOING OUT AFTER THIS, YOU'LL HAVE *PARTIES*, YOU'LL CELEBRATE YOUR *ACCOMPLISHMENTS*.

YOU *SHOULD*. YOU'VE *EARNED* IT.

GONNA GO OUT IN THE *WORLD* AND MAKE A *DIFFERENCE*.

WHATEVER YOU *DO*, REMEMBER THAT. YOU'RE GOING TO MAKE A *DIFFERENCE*.

A LOT OF TIMES IT WON'T BE *HUGE*, IT WON'T BE *VISIBLE*, EVEN.

BUT IT WILL *MATTER*, JUST THE *SAME*.

DON'T DO IT FOR *PRAISE* OR *MONEY*, THAT'S WHAT I WANT TO TELL YOU.

DO IT BECAUSE IT *NEEDS* TO BE *DONE*. DO IT TO MAKE YOUR *WORLD* BETTER.

IT'S *FINISHED*.

"...JUST A *LITTLE* AT A *TIME*..."

HE'S ON THE *ROOF*.

HE WON'T BE A *PROBLEM*.

--FOUND HIM ON THE *ROOF* TRYING TO ALTER THE *AIR CONDITIONER*, FREEZE EVERYONE PRESENT. YOU-KNOW-WHO STOPPED HIM.

OKAY, RENEE... THANKS... I'M GOING *HOME* NOW.

THERE'S SOMETHING ELSE.

THE *FEDS* CALLED... THEY FOUND THE *LEWIS* KID.

SHE *DIDN'T MAKE* IT.

...HELL...

YEAH.

...DAMN IT ALL TO HELL...

...AND *DAMN* YOU, TOO.

The END

JUNE 24th-- 6:45 P.M....

--NO... NO... I'M NOT FEEDING YOU A LINE OF BULL HERE...

YOU'VE BEEN A COP FOR OVER 20 YEARS AND YOU DON'T *BELIEVE* THE BAD GUYS ARE EVIL?

SO, THAT GUY WE BUSTED LAST WEEK FOR RAPING HIS DAUGHTER, *THAT GUY*--

YOU'RE TWISTING MY WORDS, JOSH... WHAT I *SAID* IS-- I DON'T THINK THE BAD GUYS, FOR THE MOST PART, *THINK* THAT THEY'RE ACTUALLY EVIL...

MOST PEOPLE THINK THEY'RE DOING THE RIGHT THING, NO MATTER *HOW* SICK IT IS...

LIKE THE GUY WITH HIS DAUGHTER... I WANTED TO BOUNCE HIM FROM THE ROOF TO THE SIDEWALK, BUT...

HE THOUGHT HE *LOVED* HER, AND THIS WAS HIS WAY OF *SHOWING* IT.

I DON'T *BUY* IT, SARGE... WHAT ABOUT GUYS LIKE *TWO-FACE*?

HE SURE AS $#!% KNOWS THE DIFFERENCE BETWEEN RIGHT AND WRONG...

NO $#!%, SHERLOCK, DENT'S A %#&@!NG SCHIZO THOUGH... I'M TALKING ABOUT YOUR REGULAR SKELS, NOT THE FREAKS AND SERIAL MURDERERS...

OKAY, SO THEN *HITLER*... HE THOUGHT *GENOCIDE* WAS THE RIGHT THING?

THAT'S IT... END OF DISCUSSION.

WHAT?

YOU KNOW THE *RULE*-- ALL DEBATE ENDS WHEN IT GETS TO HITLER...

OH, YEAH, I *FORGOT*...

LIKE HELL YOU DID.

--JUST *DON'T* LIKE IT, THAT'S ALL, WE'RE A *TEAM* AND--

IT'S TWO OR THREE DAYS, NATE... *BUCK UP,* OKAY?

DRIVER HERE ALREADY?

YEAH, HE'S TALKING TO THE PROBE RIGHT NOW.

*HUNH...*YOU'D THINK HE'D TAKE AT LEAST A *DAY...*

--DON'T MIND TELLING YOU, DETECTIVE, IF I HAD *MY WAY* YOU'D BE ON *PERSONAL TIME* FOR A FEW *WEEKS...*

BUT YOU'VE GOT THE *COMMISSIONER* BACKING YOU ON THIS ONE, SO...

...YOU'VE GOT THE *CASE.*

GOOD, WHO'M I PARTNERING WITH?

IT'S YOU AND ROMY CHANDLER, SHE'S GOOD AT LIAISONING WITH THE FEDS...

CROWE'S OUT SICK, SO I'M PAIRING PATTON WITH SARGE ON THIS *FIREBUG* CASE...

I THOUGHT THAT WAS *BACK-BURNED WEEKS* AGO. NO LEADS...

IT *WAS,* THEN TODAY'S PAPER CAME OUT...

SOME *TOURIST* SNAPPED A *PICTURE* LAST NIGHT, WHILE *WE* WERE ALL BASKING IN THE GLORY OF THE *FREEZE* TAKE-DOWN...

SO NOW WE GOT THE *MEDIA* UP OUR BUTT ON THIS FREAK, AND THE MAYOR WANTS IT BACK TO *TOP PRIORITY.*

REPORT: ECONOMY ON

Gotham Gaze

FIREBUG IS BACK

MOTIVE PART ONE

WRITER **ED BRUBAKER** ARTIST **MICHAEL LARK**
LETTERER **WILLIE SCHUBERT** COLORIST **NOELLE GIDDINGS**
SEPARATOR **ZYLONOL**
ASSISTANT EDITOR **NACHIE CASTRO** EDITOR **MATT IDELSON**

IT'S ALWAYS *SOMETHING,* ISN'T IT?

I'M BEGINNING TO THINK *SO...*

HOW ARE YOUR HANDS?

SORE... BUT THEY'RE HEALING...

I REALLY *DO* WISH YOU'D TAKE SOME *TIME,* MARCUS...LOSING A *PARTNER,* IT--

I KNOW... I JUST NEED TO DO THIS *ONE* CASE, AND THEN I *WILL,* LIEUTENANT.

I *MEAN* IT.

SO, YOU GOT THE WORD?

JUST BEFORE YOU DID... YOU READY TO ROLL?

JUST LET ME CHANGE REAL QUICK...

THE FEEBS ARE HOLDING A COPY OF THE FILE FOR US AT THE SCENE...

TRY NOT TO ACTUALLY CALL THEM THAT WHEN WE GET THERE, OKAY?

YOU WATCH HER BACK ON THIS, DRIVER... ROMY'S MY PARTNER.

I'LL MEET YOU IN THE CAR.

REAL THOUGHTFUL, BUTTHEAD!

HEY! I DIDN'T MEAN IT LIKE THAT...

YOU DON'T HAVE TO BE SUCH AN IDIOT ALL THE TIME, NATE...

AW, ROMY, I DIDN'T...

...DAMN IT.

OBS ON			2002
ON	FIELDS	DRIVER	WARRANTS
20 DY S A	016 LEWIS	009 LEVITZ	SCHRECK
		023 CARLIN	IDELSON
		167 KAHN	CASTRO
		178 LUTES	BOND
		233 JOHNS	BENDIS
		246 CHANG	DENNIS
		268 HART	STEWART
		285 GAUDIANO	
		298 PHILLIPS	

I SHOULD'VE COME STRAIGHT OUT LAST NIGHT WHEN THEY FOUND HER.

DAMN FEDS... I CAN'T TELL JACK FROM THESE PICTURES...

POLICE LINE DO NO

WE CAN GO BACK TO CENTRAL AND WATCH THE CRIME SCENE VIDEO...

LATER.

SO, YOU WANNA GET ME UP TO SPEED? YOU AND FIELDS WERE WORKING THIS AS A KIDNAPPING, RIGHT?

YEAH, CAUGHT IT EARLY LAST FRIDAY NIGHT.

BONNIE LEWIS, AGE FOURTEEN, DISAPPEARED ON THE WAY HOME FROM A BABY-SITTING GIG THE NIGHT BEFORE.

HALFWAY THROUGH THE NEXT DAY HER DAD GETS FAXED A RANSOM NOTE...

KIDNAPPERS WANT HALF A MILLION DOLLARS IF HE WANTS TO SEE HIS DAUGHTER AGAIN...

THEN NOTHING...

WHAT DO YOU MEAN?

THEY NEVER MADE CONTACT AGAIN.

WHO FOUND THE BODY?

LET'S SEE... TWO TEENAGERS...

APPARENTLY THEY WERE USING THE SEWER SYSTEM AS A SHORT CUT TO THE WHARF...

SO, WHAT'D YOU *THINK*? THE KIDNAPPERS KILL HER BY ACCIDENT AND JUST *DUMP* HER?

MAYBE... THOUGH IT SEEMS LIKE THEY'D STILL GO FOR THE *RANSOM* ANYWAY...

TRUE.

WERE YOU GUYS ABLE TO TRACK THE RANSOM FAX AT ALL?

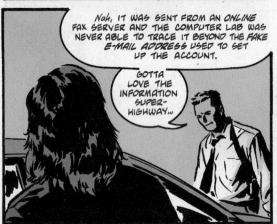

Nah, IT WAS SENT FROM AN *ONLINE* FAX SERVER AND THE COMPUTER LAB WAS NEVER ABLE TO TRACE IT BEYOND THE *FAKE E-MAIL ADDRESS* USED TO SET UP THE ACCOUNT.

GOTTA LOVE THE INFORMATION SUPER-HIGHWAY...

SO WHAT *NOW?* YOU LEARN ANYTHING HERE?

I JUST WANTED TO GET A LOOK AT THE SCENE... SEE IF IT MEANT ANYTHING.

SEEMS LIKE IT'S JUST AN *OUT OF THE WAY* SPOT, LIKE A MILLION OTHERS IN THE CITY...

LET'S GO SEE THE M.E.

GET SOME FACTS!

KANE COUNTY MORGUE

--AND FINALLY, HERE'S WHAT *DID* IT...

...YOU CAN SEE IT PRETTY CLEARLY...

BLUNT FORCE *TRAUMA* TO THE BACK OF THE HEAD.

YEAH, *ick*...

ANY IDEA WHAT SHE WAS HIT WITH?

SOMETHING *METALLIC,* HARD...

NOT *SURE* WHAT, BUT WE PULLED A COUPLE OF MICRO-SCOPIC FRAGMENTS OUT OF HER SCALP AND SENT THEM FOR ANALYSIS...

...WHATEVER IT WAS, THE *EDGE* WAS *ROUNDED*...

ANY CHANCE SHE FELL? WHACKED HER HEAD ON SOME-THING?

AN ENGINE BLOCK OR SOME-THING?

NO, THE *ANGLE* IS WRONG... UNLESS SHE WAS DOING A *BACK FLIP* AT THE TIME.

NO, YOU'RE LOOKING FOR SOMEONE *STRONG,* BETWEEN FIVE AND SIX FEET TALL...

BETWEEN *FIVE* AND *SIX* FEET?

CAN YOU *NARROW* IT DOWN A LITTLE MORE, BILL?

SORRY, BEST I CAN DO BECAUSE OF THE ANGLE OF THE BLOW.

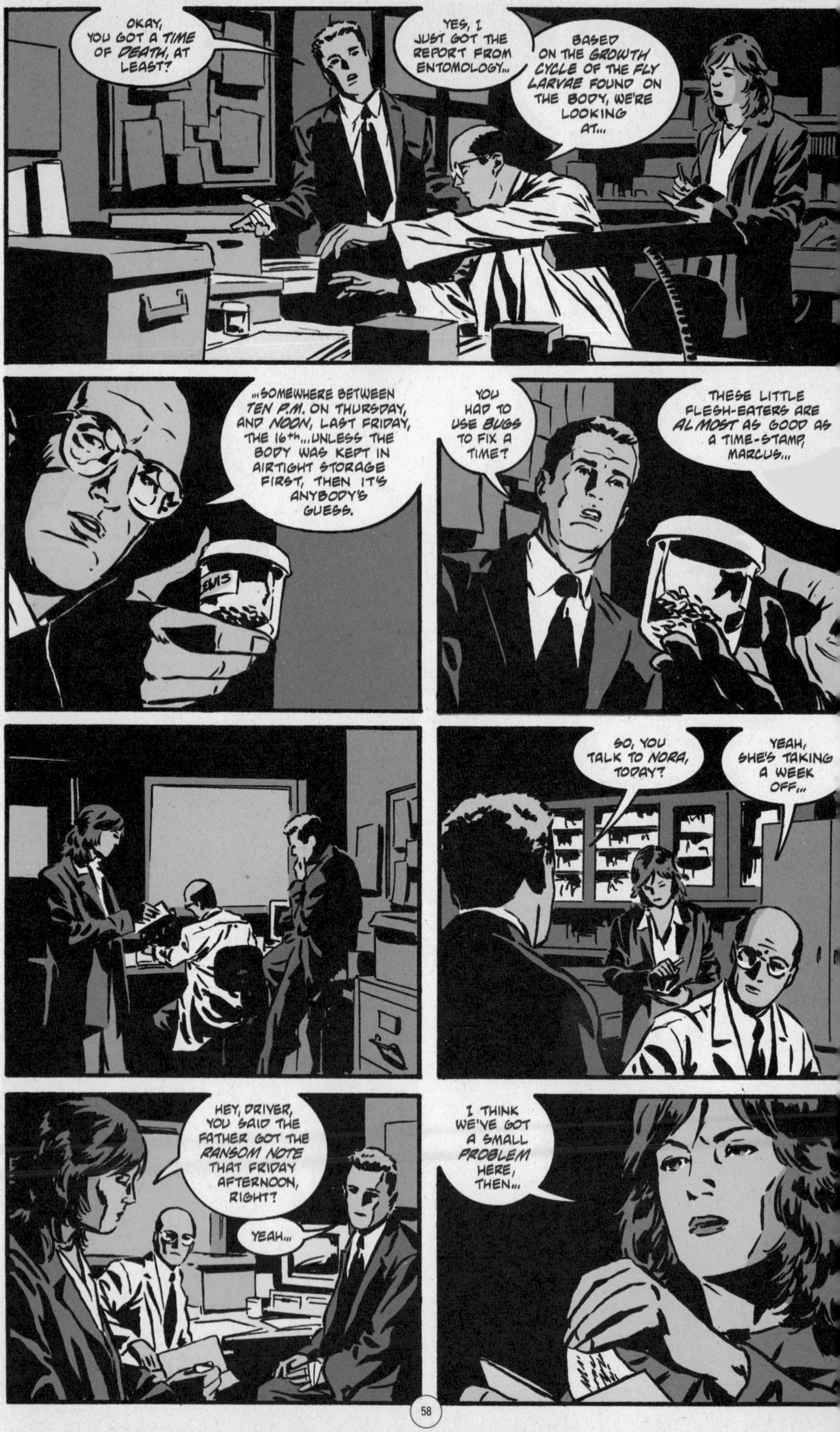
OKAY, YOU GOT A TIME OF DEATH, AT LEAST?
YES, I JUST GOT THE REPORT FROM ENTOMOLOGY...
BASED ON THE GROWTH CYCLE OF THE FLY LARVAE FOUND ON THE BODY, WE'RE LOOKING AT...
...SOMEWHERE BETWEEN TEN P.M. ON THURSDAY, AND NOON, LAST FRIDAY, THE 16th... UNLESS THE BODY WAS KEPT IN AIRTIGHT STORAGE FIRST, THEN IT'S ANYBODY'S GUESS.
YOU HAD TO USE BUGS TO FIX A TIME?
THESE LITTLE FLESH-EATERS ARE ALMOST AS GOOD AS A TIME-STAMP, MARCUS...
SO, YOU TALK TO NORA, TODAY?
YEAH, SHE'S TAKING A WEEK OFF...
HEY, DRIVER, YOU SAID THE FATHER GOT THE RANSOM NOTE THAT FRIDAY AFTERNOON, RIGHT?
YEAH...
I THINK WE'VE GOT A SMALL PROBLEM HERE, THEN...

SO, WHAT DOES *THAT* MEAN?

THAT SHE WAS ALREADY DEAD *BEFORE* HER DAD GOT THE RANSOM FAX.

SO, IT'S LIKELY THE FAX WAS JUST A *DIVERSION*, TO THROW US OFF IN THE WRONG DIRECTION.

ESPECIALLY SINCE THEY NEVER SENT A FOLLOW-UP WITH THE MONEY DROP DETAILS.

SO, WHAT IS IT, THEN? CRIME OF PASSION?

I DON'T KNOW... THE M.E. SAYS THERE WAS NO SIGN OF RAPE. IT LOOKS LIKE SOMEONE JUST KILLED HER AND DUMPED HER.

SO, BASICALLY, WE'RE BACK AT SQUARE ONE...

ANY CHANCE THAT THE *FATHER* SENT THIS RANSOM NOTE *HIMSELF?*

MY GUT SAYS *NO*... BUT WE'RE GONNA MEET WITH THE PARENTS AGAIN TOMORROW...

IF THIS *WAS* A MURDER FROM THE START WE NEED TO LOOK AT HER *PERSONAL LIFE* HARDER.

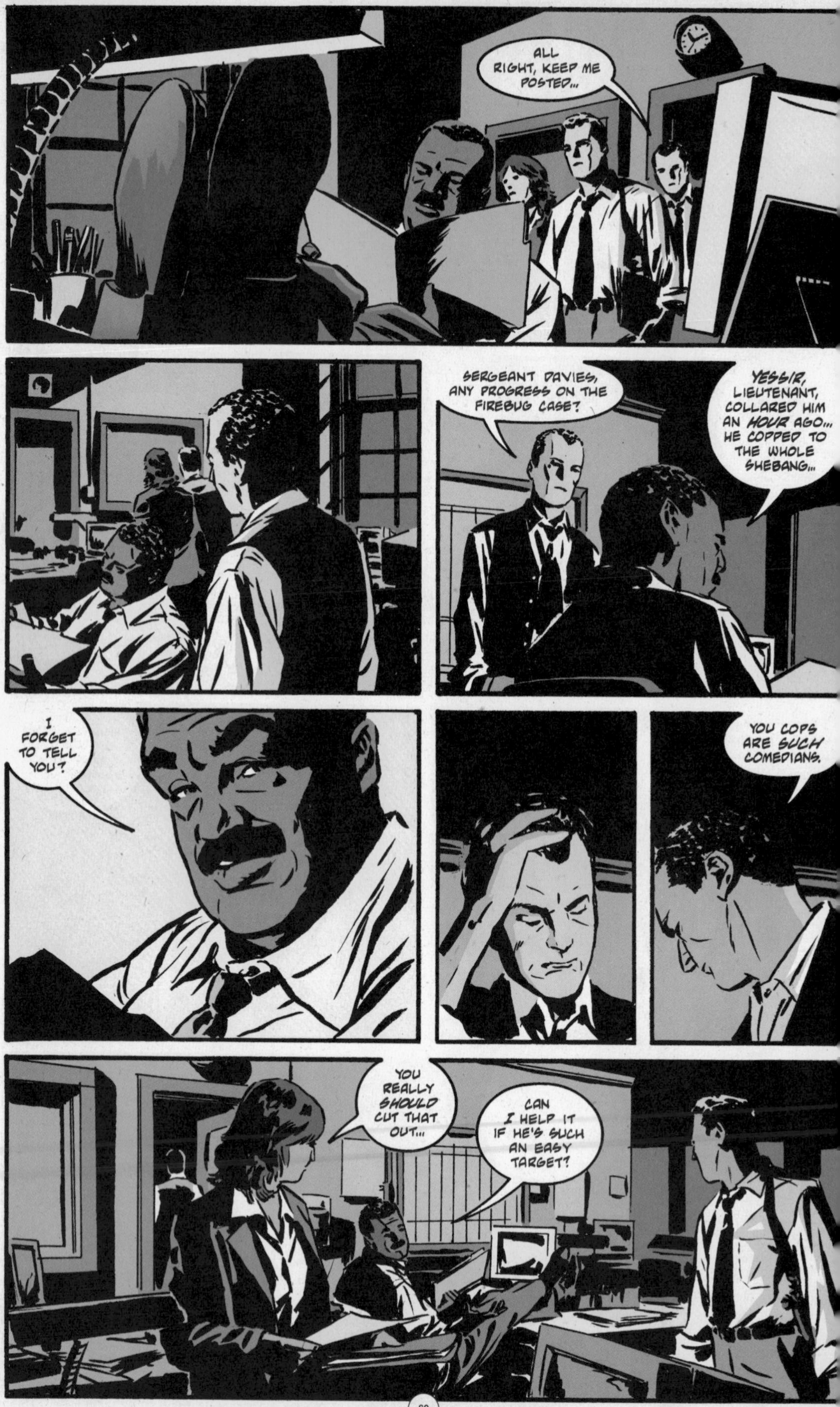
ALL RIGHT, KEEP ME POSTED...
SERGEANT DAVIES, ANY PROGRESS ON THE FIREBUG CASE?
YESSIR, LIEUTENANT, COLLARED HIM AN HOUR AGO... HE COPPED TO THE WHOLE SHEBANG...
I FORGET TO TELL YOU?
YOU COPS ARE SUCH COMEDIANS.
YOU REALLY SHOULD CUT THAT OUT...
CAN I HELP IT IF HE'S SUCH AN EASY TARGET?

JUNE 25th -- 6:10 P.M. ...

I'M AFRAID I DON'T UNDERSTAND ...?

THERE *WAS* NO KIDNAPPING?

THAT'S WHAT IT LOOKS LIKE RIGHT NOW...

SO, WE NEED TO ASK YOU SOME MORE QUESTIONS ABOUT YOUR DAUGHTER, AND HAVE ANOTHER LOOK AT HER ROOM...

OF COURSE, BUT... I THOUGHT...

SO DID *WE,* THAT'S WHAT THE KILLER WANTED.

WAS THERE ANY-ONE IN YOUR DAUGHTER'S LIFE THAT SHE WAS HAVING PROBLEMS WITH? OR MAYBE SCARED OF?

YOU THINK IT WAS SOMEONE WHO SHE *KNEW*?

MOST MURDERS *AREN'T* COMMITTED BY STRANGERS, MISTER LEWIS...

BUT... BONNIE WAS *POPULAR,* EVERYBODY LIKED HER...

...NO...

TWO BOYS AT SCHOOL... *MIKE SENDELBACH*, FROM THE NEIGHBORHOOD, WAS ONE OF THEM...

THEY WERE BOTHERING BONNIE... BULLYING HER...

SHE CAME HOME CRYING ABOUT IT A FEW WEEKS AGO...

WHAT? I NEVER HEARD ABOUT THIS...

IT DIDN'T SEEM LIKE ALL THAT BIG A DEAL... KIDS GET BULLIED...

DID BONNIE KEEP A *DIARY*, OR A JOURNAL? IF SO, WE'LL NEED IT...

NO, SHE WASN'T THE--

YES.

I'LL SHOW YOU WHERE SHE KEPT IT...

I'M REALLY SORRY, MISTER LEWIS... FOR HOW THIS TURNED OUT...

WE... WE NEVER SHOULD'VE LET HER *WALK HOME* FROM HER SITTING JOBS... IT'S JUST...

...THIS IS USUALLY SUCH A SAFE NEIGHBORHOOD...

SO, WHERE IS THIS PLACE BONNIE WAS WALKING *FROM?* THE COMBSES' HOUSE?

IT'S ABOUT A THREE-BLOCK WALK, JUST ON THE OTHER SIDE OF THE PARK...

I'LL SHOW YOU... I WANT TO TALK TO THEM AGAIN ANYWAY.

WHAT'D YOU GET FROM THE BEDROOM?

DIARY, SCHOOL YEARBOOK A COUPLE PHOTO ALBUMS...

JUST COVERING THE BASES...

THIS REALLY IS A PRETTY NICE NEIGHBORHOOD, Y'KNOW?

A BIT OUT OF YOUR *PRICE RANGE,* I THINK, ROMY...

$#!%... WHAT *ISN'T?*

Ah...WHO WANTS TO LIVE NEXT TO A BUNCH OF *INTERNET MILLIONAIRES,* ANYWAY?

DON'T EVEN GET ME STARTED...

IS THIS YOU?

OH, THAT... YES. THAT'S AT A FEW THOUSAND FEET. HAVE YOU EVER DONE ANY SKY-DIVING, DETECTIVE CHANDLER?

I'M A POLICE OFFICER, MISTER COMBS. THAT'S DANGEROUS ENOUGH FOR ME...

IT'S QUITE A RUSH, HONESTLY.

SO, NOW, WHAT DID YOU WANT TO KNOW, DETECTIVE DRIVER? I CAN'T IMAGINE THAT WE HAVE MUCH TO ADD TO OUR ORIGINAL STATEMENTS...

WELL, WE'RE APPROACHING THE CASE FROM A DIFFERENT ANGLE NOW, SO I'M AFRAID I'LL HAVE TO TAKE A LITTLE MORE OF YOUR TIME...

BONNIE'S FATHER SAID SHE ALWAYS WALKED HOME FROM BABY-SITTING. DO YOU KNOW WHAT PATH SHE TOOK?

AS I SAID BEFORE, SHE WENT THROUGH THE PARK...

AND THAT NIGHT SHE LEFT AT *WHAT* TIME?

WELL, WE GOT HOME AT A LITTLE AFTER NINE, SO IT WAS A FEW MINUTES AFTER THAT. AROUND 9:15...

AND YOU DIDN'T THINK THAT WAS A LITTLE *LATE* FOR A FOURTEEN-YEAR-OLD GIRL TO BE TAKING A WALK IN THE PARK?

NOT *ESPECIALLY*...

THIS ISN'T THE EAST END, AFTER ALL...

THE PARK ONLY EVEN HAS *ONE* HOMELESS PERSON, AND BONNIE WAS *FRIENDS* WITH HIM. SHE USED TO BRING HIM FOOD.

IS *THAT* RIGHT? YOU GOT A NAME FOR THIS *HOMELESS* PERSON?

I'M SURE I'VE *HEARD* IT BEFORE, BUT I WOULDN'T KNOW...

DID BONNIE *EVER* TALK TO YOU ABOUT HER PERSONAL LIFE? PROBLEMS AT SCHOOL, OR...?

OF COURSE NOT. SHE WAS OUR SITTER, SHE DIDN' CONFIDE IN US.

I REALLY DON'T SEE HOW THIS CAN POSSIBLY--

SOMEONE SMASHED IN THE BACK OF BONNIE LEWIS' SKULL NOT LONG AFTER SHE WALKED OUT YOUR DOOR, MISTER COMBS...

NOW, I'M SORRY IF IT'S AN INCONVENIENCE TO YOU, BUT I'M TRYING TO FIND OUT WHO THAT WAS.

I JUST DON'T SEE HOW WE CAN HELP...

BONNIE... SHE WAS JUST GOOD WITH JOHNATHAN... SHE WAS A GOOD SITTER...

LOOK, IF THERE'S NOTHING ELSE... WE REALLY DO HAVE TO GET TO JOHNATHAN'S CHESS MATCH...

HOW LONG ARE WE GOING TO WAIT FOR THIS SUPPOSED HOMELESS GUY, MARCUS?

WHAT? YOU DOUBT HIS EXISTENCE?

CONSIDERING MARIE COMBS IS THE SOURCE, I'D BE *SURPRISED* IF HE WASN'T JUST SOME *HIPPIE* WHO COMES BY TO FEED PIGEONS...

SHE SEES SOME GUY WITH LONG HAIR, ASSUMES HE'S A *BUM* LIVING IN THE PARK.

YEAH, FOR THE LAST PEOPLE TO SEE THE GIRL *ALIVE*, THEY DON'T SEEM TOO SHOOK UP ABOUT IT...

PROBABLY MORE WORRIED ABOUT FINDING A NEW SITTER FOR LITTLE BOBBY FISHER...

WISH THEY COULD'VE BEEN MORE HELP, ANYWAY...

BEEN OVER A WEEK, AND WE STILL HAVE *NO IDEA* WHY ANYONE WOULD WANT TO *HURT* THIS LITTLE GIRL.

OH, MY GOD...

WHAT? WHAT'D YOU FIND?

OH, SORRY. I JUST CAN'T BELIEVE KIDS STILL WRITE, "HAVE A BITCHIN' SUMMER" IN YEARBOOKS.

THAT'S LIKE WRITING "*WARMEST REGARDS*" OR SOMETHING... IT'S SO SAD...

I'M REALLY GLAD I SURVIVED HIGH SCHOOL.

WHAT?

NOTHING.

OH, HEY, CHECK IT *OUT*... HERE'S THAT LITTLE JERK BONNIE'S *MOM* WAS TALKING ABOUT...

LEMME SEE...

WHAT DO YOU *THINK?* A YOUNG TED BUNDY?

LIKE WE'RE GONNA GET *THAT* LUCKY...

~~zzt~~ ALL UNITS RESPOND...

ARSON FIRE AT 45TH AND SPRANG... SUSPECT *FIREBUG* BEING PURSUED BY OFFICERS... ALL UNITS RESPOND...

THAT'S LIKE, TWO MINUTES FROM HERE...

I *KNOW*...

WHEEOOOWHEEOO

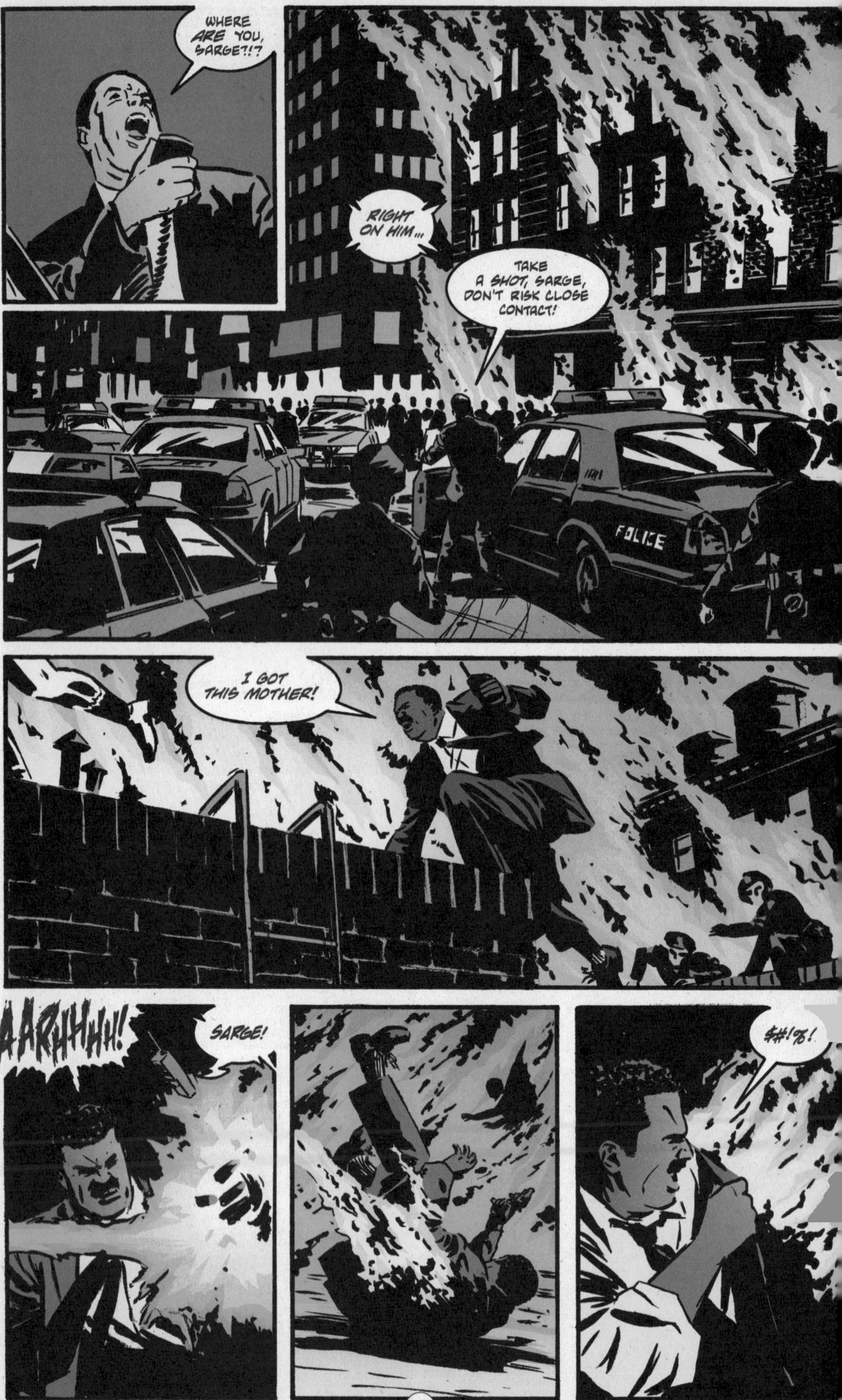
WHERE ARE YOU, SARGE?!?
RIGHT ON HIM...
TAKE A SHOT, SARGE, DON'T RISK CLOSE CONTACT!
POLICE
I GOT THIS MOTHER!
AARHHHH!
SARGE!
$#!%!

DAMN IT!

SARGE! YOU ALL RIGHT?

NO. DAMN IT... I LOST HIM...

DAMN IT ALL TO HELL!

NATE!

WHAT CAN WE DO?

IS THERE ANYBODY IN THE APARTMENT HOUSE STILL?

I DON'T KNOW. WE'VE BEEN EVACUATING...FIRE TRUCKS SHOULD BE HERE ANY TIME.

WHY AREN'T THEY HERE ALREADY?

DAMN IT... I'M GOING IN...

WAIT--

SKAAAASSH!

WHAT THE HELL...?

tnnnk

YOU'RE OKAY. NOW GO TO THE OTHER SIDE OF THE STREET.

DETECTIVE DRIVER...

THAT'S THE LAST OF THE TENANTS...

WHO *WAS* THAT MASKED MAN?

STOP IT.

FINALLY...

I GOTTA FIND SARGE, I THINK HE MIGHT'VE GOT *HURT*...

YOU WANNA HELP?

SURE...

CAN YOU HOLD DOWN THE FORT HERE, DRIVER?

YEAH, DON'T SWEAT IT.

I'LL FIND YOU TWO LATER.

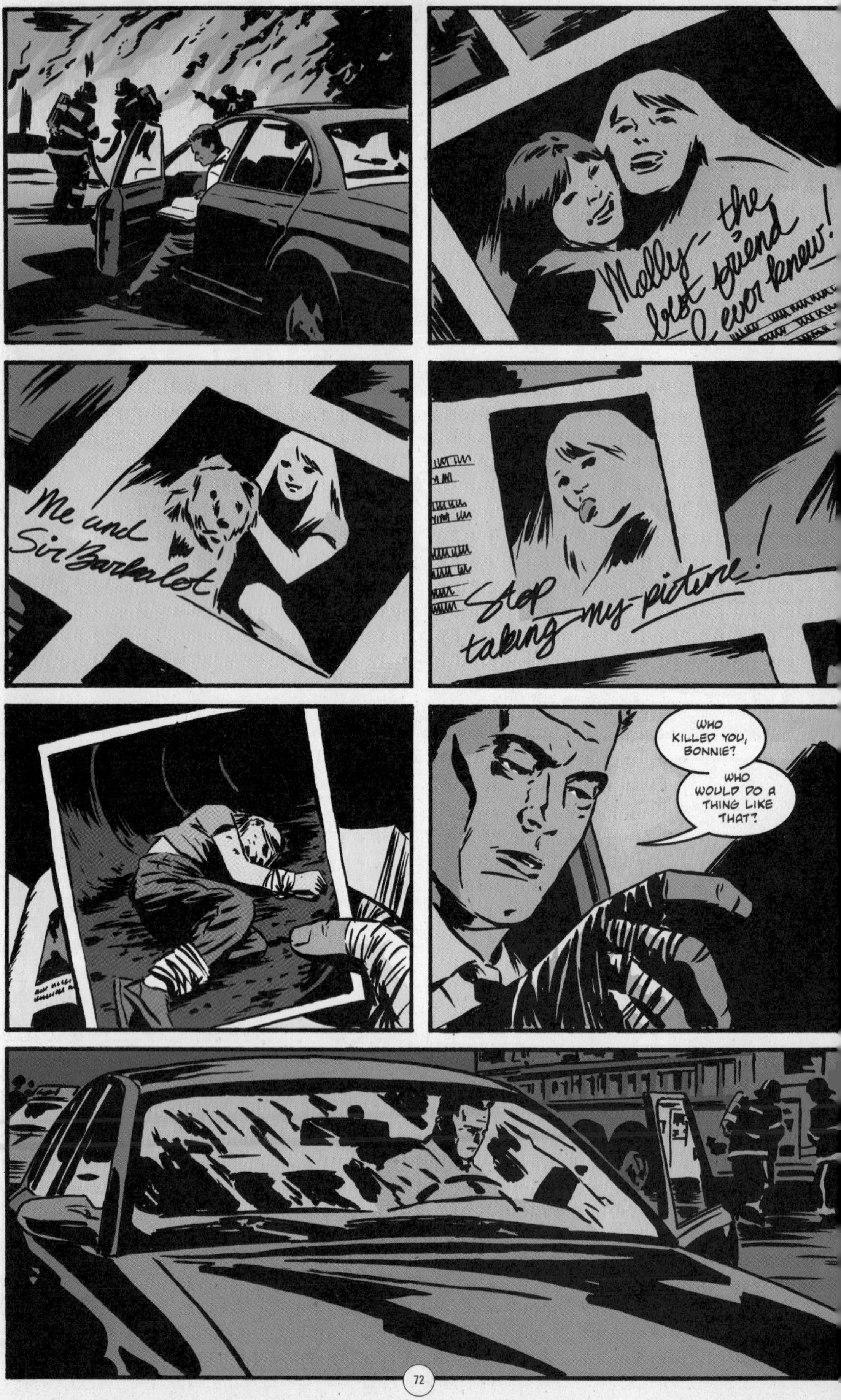
Molly - the best friend I ever knew!
Me and Sir Barkalot
Stop taking my picture!
WHO KILLED YOU, BONNIE?
WHO WOULD DO A THING LIKE THAT?

JUNE 26th, 6:03 p.m....

..'N SUDDENLY SHE'S ALL UPTIGHT.

"DON'T SWEAR IN FRONT OF MY CHILDREN."

AND I'M LIKE, LADY, THAT AIN'T EVEN SWEARING....

WELL, MAYBE SHE WAS CATHOLIC.

PROBABLY, BUT, I MEAN, THAT WASN'T EVEN HIS REAL NAME... HIS NAME WAS JOSHUA...

SHE'S ALL IN MY FACE ABOUT A GREEK TRANSLATION.

HIS NAME WAS JOSH CHRIST?

NAW, HE WAS LIKE JOSH LIPSHITZ OR SOMETHING, SOME JEWISH NAME...

CHRIST JUST MEANS MESSIAH...

Hmm.... HOW DO YOU KNOW ALL THIS, SERGEANT DAVIES?

BECAUSE I'M A DETECTIVE, I INVESTIGATE THINGS.

IT'S MY NATURE.

DON'T LISTEN TO HIM, STACY... HE'S JUST BONING UP FOR THINGS TO TALK ABOUT WHEN HE'S SPENDING ETERNITY IN A LAKE OF FIRE...

LIKE ALL LAPSED CATHOLICS.

YEAH, *RIGHT*... I'LL SEND YOU A POSTCARD WHEN I GET THERE, AZEVEDA...

ALL RIGHT...

GUESS I'M NOT GONNA WAIT FOR *PATTON* ANYMORE.

GOTTA GIVE *THE PROBE* AN UPDATE ON THIS FIREBUG FIASCO...

ANYTHING HAPPENING?

NOT SINCE I GOT MY *BEST JACKET* TOASTED LAST NIGHT...

HAVE A GOOD *SHIFT*, DETECTIVES...

SEE YA, STACY...

HEY, STACY...

OH, HI, NATE...

SARGE WAS JUST LOOKING FOR YOU.

YEAH, I STOPPED TO GRAB SOME CHINESE...

ROMY UP THERE?

NO, SHE AND DETECTIVE DRIVER ALREADY CAME AND WENT... THEY GOT A LEAD ON THE *LEWIS* CASE, I THINK...

SO WHAT DO *YOU* THINK?

IS IT ANYTHING, OR JUST TEEN GIRL ANGST?

WELL, THIS POEM SHE WROTE--DIFFERENT COLORS, MADE OF TEARS -- THAT'S DEFINITELY TEEN GIRL ANGST.

NO, I'M TALKING ABOUT THE STUFF ABOUT THESE *PUNKS*...

MOTIVE PART TWO

WRITER **ED BRUBAKER** ARTIST **MICHAEL LARK**

LETTERER **WILLIE SCHUBERT** COLORIST **NOELLE GIDDINGS**

SEPARATOR **ZYLONOL**

ASSISTANT EDITOR **NACHIE CASTRO** EDITOR **MATT IDELSON**

YEAH, I THINK IT'S SOMETHING, BUT COULD SHE BE MORE VAGUE?

"MIKE S. AND HIS STUPID FRIEND BRIAN KEEP BEING AFTER ME. NO MATTER WHERE I GO ON CAMPUS, THEY FIND ME.

"THEY SAY THEY'RE GOING TO TAKE IT.

"I NEVER SHOULD HAVE GONE WITH MIKE BEHIND THE BLEACHERS THAT DAY."

IT'S NOT VAGUE, YOU *KNOW* WHAT THEY'RE AFTER...

I DON'T THINK THAT'S IT. SHE CAME HOME CRYING ABOUT THESE GUYS, ACCORDING TO HER MOM...

I DON'T THINK SHE'D'VE HID A *RAPE* ATTEMPT FROM HER.

SO, WHAT, THEN?

I DON'T KNOW. HERE'S SOMETHING ELSE, THOUGH, FROM A MONTH AGO...

"MRS. K. IS A TOTAL %.!@$%! SHE SAID SHE'S GOING TO TELL MY OTHER CUSTOMERS ABOUT ME.

"I TOLD HER I'D TELL THEM ABOUT HER IF SHE DID. MOLLY WAS SO PROUD OF ME."

YEAH, I SAW THAT, TOO... WHAT'D YOU THINK?

SOUNDS LIKE MAYBE OUR LITTLE ANGEL WASN'T SO SWEET AFTER ALL...

THEY NEVER ARE, ROMY...

YO! TOSS THAT PILL, DOG! I'M OPEN!

OKAY, THERE'S MIKE SENDELBACH...

YOU GOT A LIKELY BRIAN?

YEAH...

HEY, BRIAN!

THAT'S HIM...

NICE.

G.C.P.D. WE NEED TO TALK TO MIKE AND BRIAN, THE REST OF YOU CAN KEEP PLAYING...

YO, WHAT'CHU WANNA TALK ABOUT?

BONNIE LEWIS.

MAYBE YOU REMEMBER HER FROM BEHIND THE BLEACHERS...

...HUH, MIKE?

GO, DOG! RUN!

SMAK!

FREEZE, YOU LITTLE BUTT-HEADS!

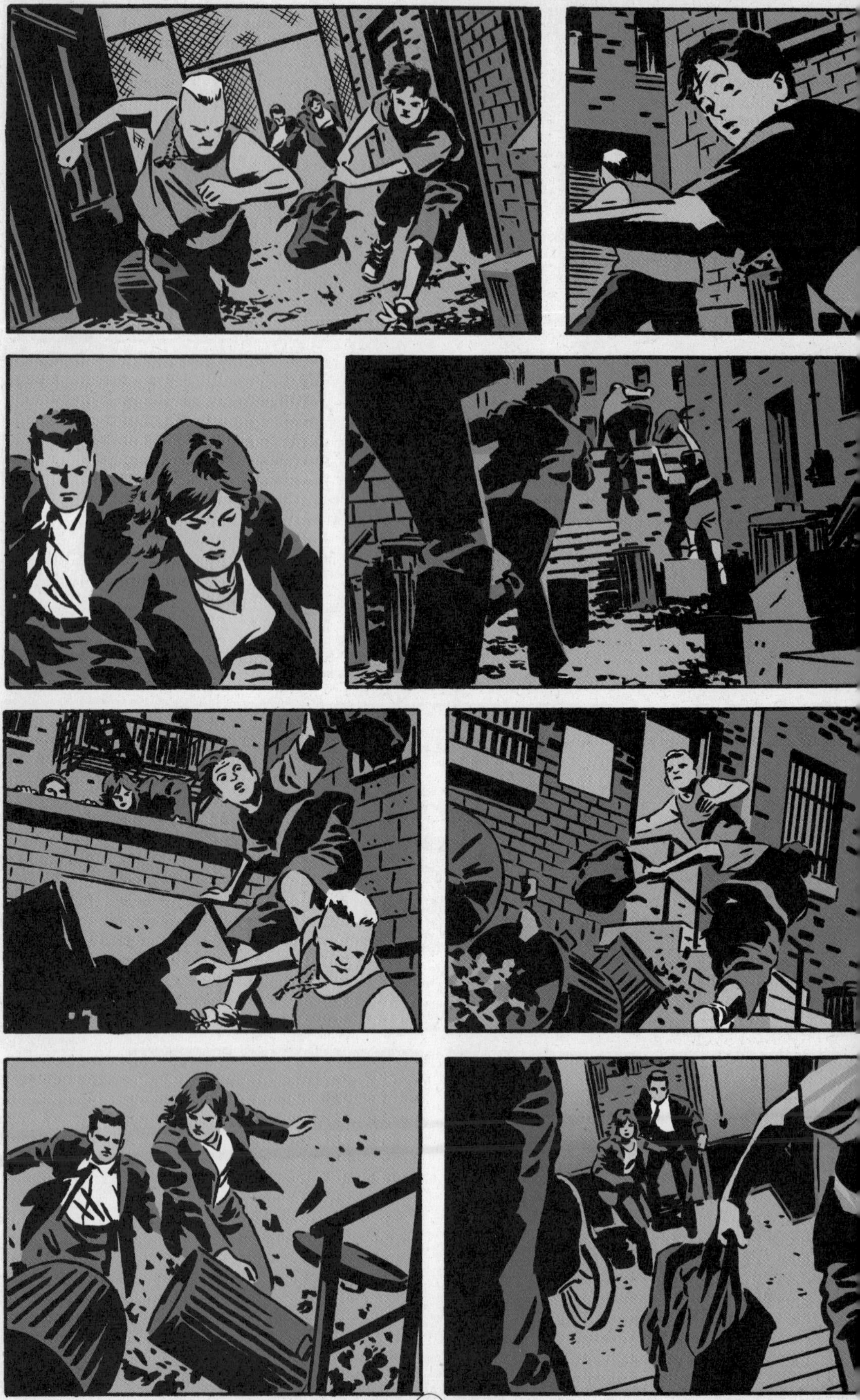

YOU OKAY?

YEAH... ...NEVER *WAS* TOO *GOOD* AT *DODGE-BALL.*

WHATTAYA THINK? HEADING FOR THE ROOF?

WHAT ELSE?

KIDS.

OKAY, THAT WAS *FUN.*

NOW HOW ABOUT YOU ANSWER OUR QUESTIONS?

WHAT? HOW DID...

SCIENCE, NITWIT.

SO, WHO WANTS TO BE FIRST TO TELL ME ABOUT BONNIE LEWIS?

WE AIN'T SAYIN' $#@% TO NO FIVE-OH.

OKAY, FINE... LET'S SEE WHAT YOUR *PARENTS* HAVE TO SAY ABOUT THAT *DOWNTOWN.*

ROOF

FOR *WHAT?* WE AIN'T DONE *NOTHIN'*!!

WRONG... *ASSAULTING AN OFFICER,* FOR STARTERS. THAT'LL GET YOU SOME TIME IN SPRANG HALL, JUVENILE DETENTION CENTER...

YOU CAN SEE HOW MUCH *REAL BROTHERS* LIKE RICH WHITE KIDS CO-OPTING THEIR CULTURE, *"DOG."*

LOOK, WE'RE SORRY, OKAY?

HERE, YOU CAN *TAKE IT...* WE DON'T...

SHUT *UP,* MIKE, KEEP YO FOOLISH MOUTH SHUT.

NO, MAN, SCREW THIS...

I CAN'T HAVE MY *MOM* GETTING A CALL FROM THE *COPS.*

I DON'T EVEN *WANT* IT ANYMORE.

AW, *MAN...*

HERE.

A BATARANG.

OKAY...

I'M SORRY, WHAT THE *HELL* DOES THIS *THING* HAVE TO DO WITH BONNIE LEWIS?

IT WAS *HERS...*

WELL, IT WAS *ROBIN'S* REALLY, BUT BONNIE SNAGGED IT.

WE'RE TALKING ABOUT ROBIN THE BOY *WONDER,* ROBIN? OF *BATMAN* AND...?

YEAH...

"A COUPLE OF MONTHS AGO ROBIN THREW DOWN WITH *KILLER CROC* AT OUR SCHOOL, ROBINSON HIGH..."

"SOME PEOPLE THINK ROBIN ACTUALLY GOES TO ROBINSON, EXCEPT THERE WAS A BASEBALL GAME THAT DAY, SO HE *MIGHT* BE FROM SPRINGER LATIN..."

"ANYWAY, IN ALL THE ACTION, HE BOUNCED A BUNCH OF BATARANGS OFF THAT SCALY MOTHER..."

"IT WAS *WICKED COOL!*"

"AND I DON'T KNOW WHEN, 'CAUSE I NEVER *SAW IT*, BUT BONNIE GRABBED ONE OF THEM WHEN NO ONE WAS LOOKING..."

"HER AND MOLLY WERE WALKING AROUND ACTING ALL *BIG* AFTER THAT, FOR NO REASON... THEN BONNIE TAKES ME BEHIND THE BLEACHERS AND SHOWS IT TO ME AND I WAS ALL, *'DAMN'*..."

JUST TO EVEN BE ABLE TO *TOUCH IT*, Y'KNOW?

AND YOU JUST *HAD* TO HAVE IT AFTER THAT, HUNH?

YO, IT'S A *BATARANG!*

KNOW HOW MUCH YOU C'N GET FOR THAT SUCKA ON G-BAY?

WE WEREN'T GONNA SELL IT...

IT'S JUST, SHE WAS A GIRL, Y'KNOW? WHAT'S SHE NEED A PIECE OF BATMAN FOR?

LEMME SEE IF I'VE GOT THIS... YOU LITTLE *JERKS KILLED* SOMEONE FOR A SOUVENIR?

KILLED? WAIT A MINUTE...

Tino's BAR & GRILL

CH

OPEN

--AND HITS DRIVER SMACK IN THE FACE.

OUCH.

ROMY TELLS IT BETTER.

NO, IT'S JUST NOT THAT *FUNNY,* NATE.

LUCKY THEY DIDN'T HAVE A GUN. KIDS TODAY.

OKAY, I GOT WHAT WE NEEDED FROM THE *BEST FRIEND.*

SHE GAVE IT UP ON THE *PHONE?*

SHE WANTS A COP COMING BY HER HOUSE TONIGHT INSTEAD? I DON'T *THINK* SO...

SO, WHAT'S THE SCOOP?

MRS. K. IS MRS. KURTZBAUM, LIVES AROUND THE CORNER FROM THE COMBS.

APPARENTLY, SHE CAUGHT BONNIE GOING THROUGH HER *CLOSET* ONE NIGHT.

BABY-SITTERS.

WHAT'D SHE FIND?

SECRETS. MRS. K. WAS IN THE CLOSET HERSELF, IT SEEMS, ALONG WITH SEVERAL PICTURES OF HER AT SOME OF GOTHAM'S SEAMIER NIGHTCLUBS...

WE TALKING ABOUT BLACK-MAIL?

COULD BE. WE'LL HAVE TO TALK TO THE WOMAN, OBVIOUSLY, SEE IF THERE WAS A GRUDGE.

SO, WAIT, THESE *KIDS* WEREN'T THE *KILLERS.*

NAH, JUST A COUPLE OF JERKS.

STOLE HER BATARANG.

SO, WHAT'S UP WITH THE *FIREBUG*? ANY WORD?

YEAH, SARGE IS GRABBING A DRINK WITH *HARVEY BULLOCK*, OF ALL PEOPLE... I GUESS BULLOCK'S GOT A SOURCE MIGHT BE ABLE TO TIP US TO THIS SKEEZE'S WHEREABOUTS...

PHHFFT-- HARVEY...

WE BETTER GET BACK OUT THERE.

YEAH, WE'VE GOT A *PARK* TO STAKE OUT...

THEY COULD BE KIND OF A CUTE COUPLE, DON'T YOU THINK?

WHAT?

WHAT?

--YOU DON'T *REALLY* THINK THAT, DO YOU?

AH, I DON'T KNOW... I GUESS *NOT.*

CHARLIE WAS LIKE THAT, THOUGH... WOULDN'T LISTEN TO ANYTHING RECORDED AFTER 1968...

SO, I HEARD THEY GOT A NEW *CHICK* COMING UP, SOME BLACK GIRL WITH AN IRISH NAME...

FIRST PERSON ON THE M.C.U. THAT WASN'T HAND-PICKED BY *JIM GORDON...* IT'S THE END OF AN ERA...

I GUESS SO...

...EXCEPT FOR THAT ONE SONG, *"OOOH CHILD..."*

WELL... THAT *IS* A GREAT SONG.

HEY, WAIT, YOU WERE THE *LAST* PERSON PICKED BY GORDON, WEREN'T YOU?

YEAH, ABOUT A MONTH OR SO BEFORE HE... BEFORE HE *RETIRED...*

CHARLIE WAS WORKING A MULTIPLE MURDER THAT CROSSED OVER WITH A ROBBERY I WAS ON, SO WE WORKED THEM TOGETHER...

TEAMED UP TO *FIGHT CRIME,* HUH?

OR AT LEAST *WHINE* ABOUT IT.

ANYWAY, HE RECOMMENDED ME TO GORDON AFTER THAT.

HEY, I THINK I *SAW* SOMETHING OVER THIS WAY.

C'MON...

ANYTHING?

Huh. THOUGHT I SAW SOME *RUSTLING*...I GUESS IT COULDA BEEN A BIRD OR SOMETHING.

THIS IS A WILD-GOOSE CHASE, MARCUS...

THERE IS NO *HOME-LESS GUY*...

YOU'RE SO *SURE?*

WELL, WHERE THE HELL *IS* HE?

DOES HE HAVE A *JOB?*

WORK THE *LATE SHIFT?*

WELL, WHAT ELSE ARE WE GONNA *DO?*

WE GOT *NOTHING*...

THIS GIRL'S JUST *DEAD*, AND *NOTHING* JUMPS OUT AT ME AND SAYS *WHY*...

I SAY WE GO DRAG *MRS. K.* OUT OF THE CLOSET AND SEE WHAT *SHE* HAS TO SAY ABOUT IT.

MAYBE WE *SHOULD*... I DUNNO...

HEY...

WHAT THE HELL IS *THIS?*

LOOKS LIKE IT WAS SOME KIND OF *FORT* OR SOMETHING...

YEAH... EMPHASIS ON *WAS*...

LOOK AT *THIS*... SOMEBODY WAS *LIVING* HERE... A BOOK... SOME CLOTHES.

THINK MAYBE THE LOCALS GOT TIRED OF THEIR OWN LITTLE HOMELESS PROBLEM?

THE TIMING'S KIND OF WEIRD, THOUGH, RIGHT AFTER THE GIRL GETS--

HEY-- HOLD IT!

UHHH...

GET OUTTA MY HOUSE!

WHAK

AH!

GET OFFA ME!

MY HOUSE!

MARCUS, COVER YOUR FACE!

SHHPPT

AARRHH!

BURNS! EVERYTHING BURNS!

KRAK

YOU REALIZE THAT WE'VE GOTTA *CARRY* THIS WALKING URINAL CAKE TO THE CAR NOW, *RIGHT?*

I *DON'T* THINK HE WOULD'VE GONE *VOLUNTARILY* ANYWAY...

AW, GOD, ROMY... HE'S DROOLIN' SNOT ALL OVER THE SEAT...

WHAT DO YOU WANT *ME* TO DO ABOUT IT?

THAT *HARLAN COMBS* JERK JUST ZOOMED BY IN AN S.U.V.

THE HELL'S *HE* GOIN' IN SUCH A HURRY THIS TIME OF NIGHT?

THAT GUY...

I WISH I COULD THINK OF A GOOD REASON TO *BOTHER* HIM AGAIN...

SOMETHING ABOUT HIM AND HIS WIFE JUST GETS UNDER YOUR SKIN, Y'KNOW?

FIRST SELF-CENTERED YUPPIES YOU EVER MET, MARCUS?

DETECTIVE CAR TWELVE COME IN...

DETECTIVE 12 HERE...

ROMY, IT'S *NATE*... WE'RE PUTTING TOGETHER A UNIT TO TAKE DOWN THIS FIREBUG DIRTBAG. YOU GUYS WANT IN?

YEAH SURE...

JUST GOTTA DROP OFF A *PACKAGE* AT CENTRAL FIRST...

...WASN'T TRYIN' TO START A FIGHT, I WAS JUST *ASKING.*

YEAH, I'M JUST GETTING *TIRED* OF THE QUESTION, I GUESS...

SO, I'LL TAKE THAT AS A NO...

TAKE IT HOWEVER YOU *WANT,* MARCUS.

EVADING THE QUESTION JUST MAKES ME THINK THERE *IS* SOMETHING GOING ON...

HE'S MY *PARTNER,* MARCUS...YOU REALLY THINK I'D SLEEP WITH MY PARTNER?

I DON'T KNOW...IT WOULDN'T BE THE *FIRST* TIME.

YOU EVER SLEEP WITH ANY OF *YOURS?*

WELL, MINE WERE ALL *GUYS*, SO...

BIGOT.

WHERE ARE WE SET UP?

THIRD FLOOR, APARTMENT C.

GOOD, YOU'RE *HERE*, WE WERE GETTING TIRED OF WAITING...

WHAT'S THE *DEAL?* WHERE IS THIS *GUY?*

HE'S RIGHT DOWN THE HALL, IN G.

LIGHTS ARE OFF, BUT THE TV'S ON SO HE'S PROBABLY UP...

SO, BULLOCK'S TIP WAS GOOD?

YEAH, HARVEY KNEW A GUY WHO KNEW A GUY WHO KNEW WHERE THIS SUCKER WAS HOLED UP...

THAT WAS *ALWAYS* HARVEY'S PROBLEM, KNEW A FEW *TOO MANY* GUYS WHO KNEW A GUY...

SHUT YOUR MOUTH!

RIGHT NOW.

I DIDN'T MEAN NOTHIN'... I SWEAR, SARGE...

HEY... ISN'T THIS PLACE KIND OF A *DUMP* FOR A FREAK WHO'S BEEN TAKIN' DOWN *SERIOUS BANK* THE LAST FEW WEEKS?

YEAH, THAT CROSSED MY MIND...

NEVER KNOW WHERE THESE SICKOS ARE GONNA HIDE OUT, THOUGH...

ENOUGH SMALL TALK...

LET'S GO BUST THIS DIRTBAG.

REMEMBER, THIS MOTHER IS *NOT* TO BE TRIFLED WITH...

HE MAKES A MOVE FOR ONE OF HIS FLAME-THROWERS... *SHOOT HIM.*

STRIKE TEAM IN POSITION, ALL UNITS MOVE IN.

WHUMP!

KRDCH!

G.C.P.D.!

JOSEPH RIGGER, YOU'RE UNDER ARREST!

PLACE YOUR HANDS SLOWLY BEHIND YOUR HEAD!

DON'T BE AN IDIOT, MAN...

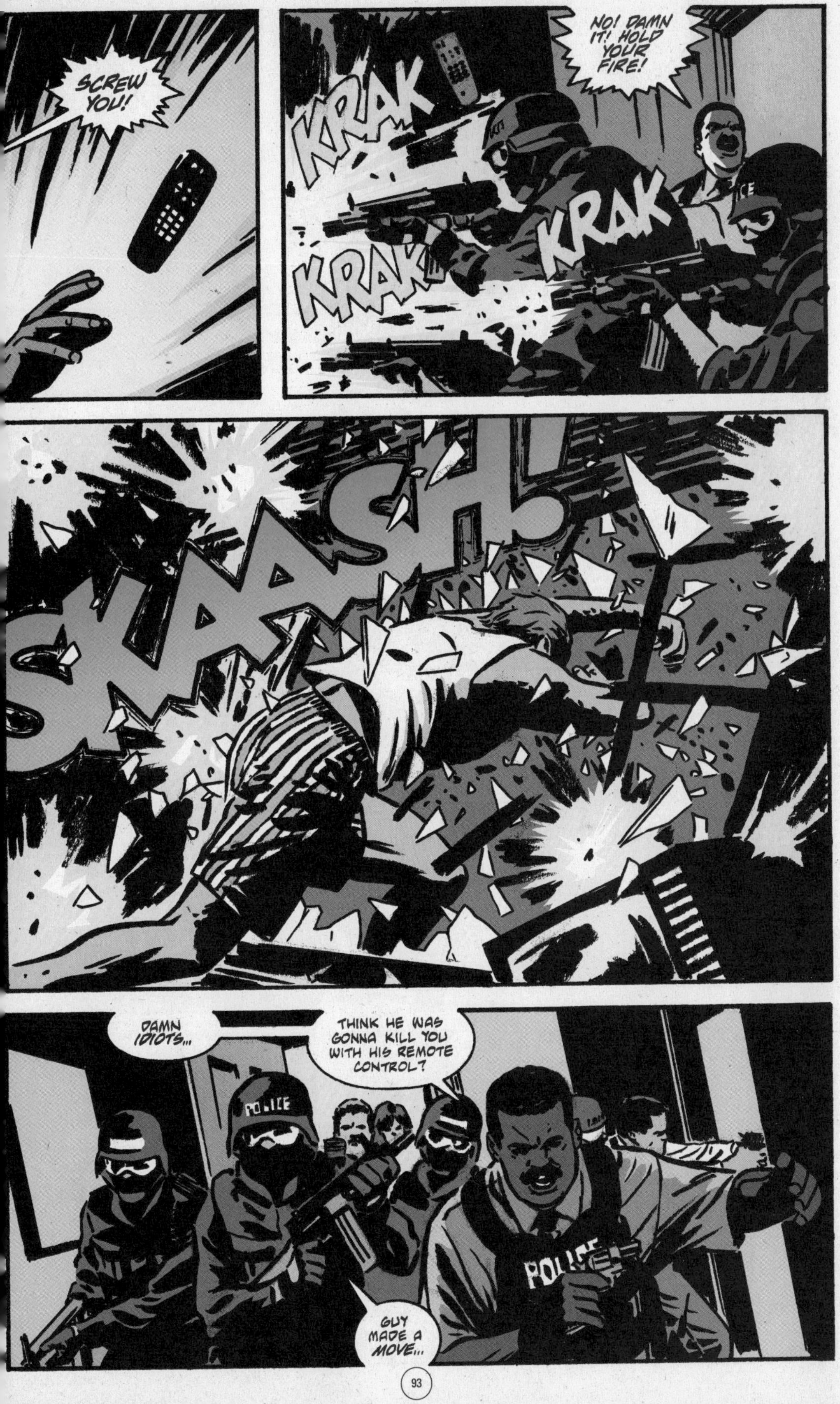
SCREW YOU!
NO! DAMN IT! HOLD YOUR FIRE!
KRAK
KRAK
KRAK
DAMN IDIOTS...
THINK HE WAS GONNA KILL YOU WITH HIS REMOTE CONTROL?
GUY MADE A MOVE...

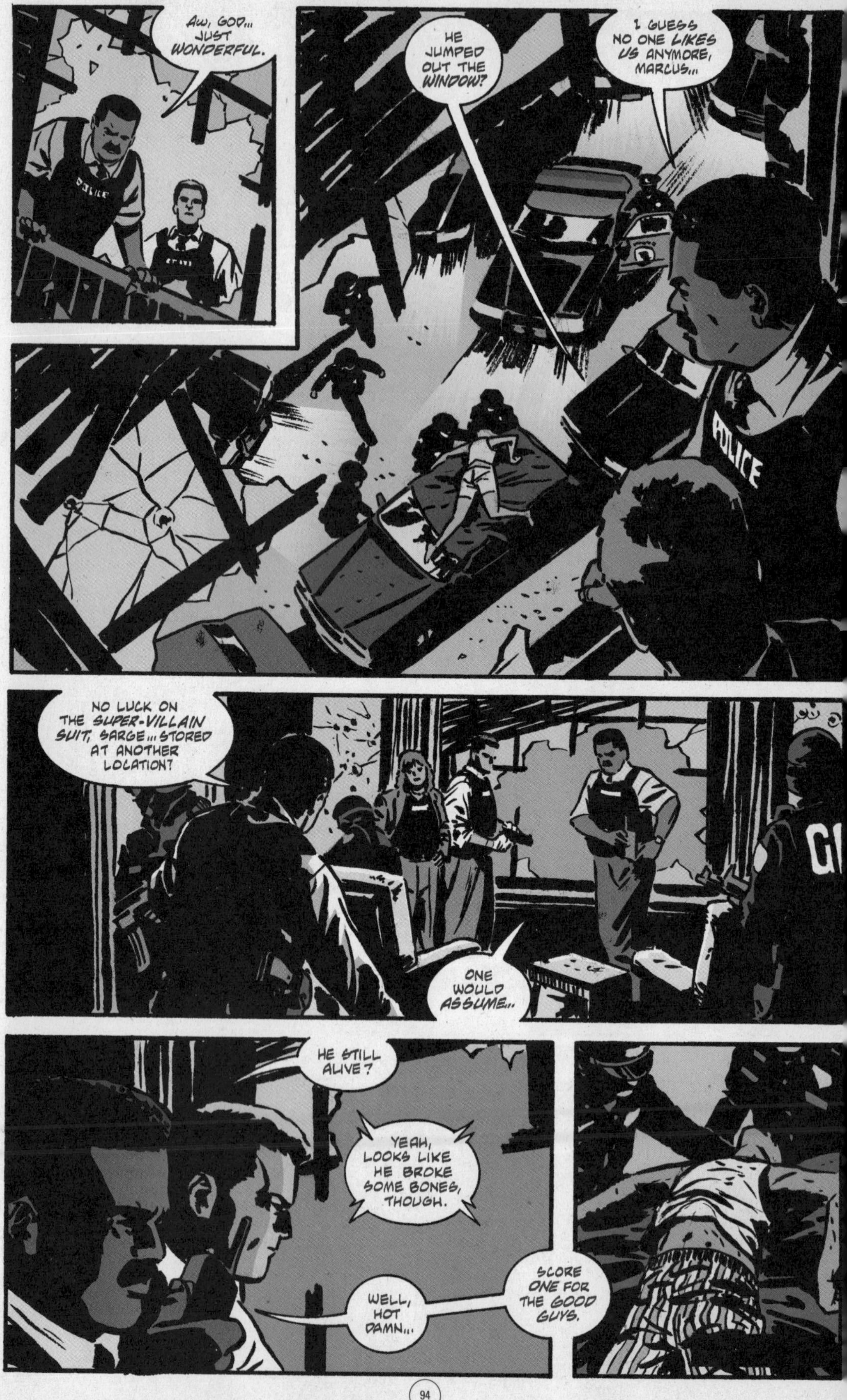
AW, GOD... JUST WONDERFUL.
HE JUMPED OUT THE WINDOW?
I GUESS NO ONE LIKES US ANYMORE, MARCUS...
POLICE
NO LUCK ON THE SUPER-VILLAIN SUIT, SARGE... STORED AT ANOTHER LOCATION?
ONE WOULD ASSUME...
HE STILL ALIVE?
YEAH, LOOKS LIKE HE BROKE SOME BONES, THOUGH.
WELL, HOT DAMN...
SCORE ONE FOR THE GOOD GUYS.

JUNE 27th, 6:45 P.M....

NO, I WAS NEVER A FULL-FLEDGED FED. JUST A CADET.

OKAY, BUT STILL WHY GIVE IT UP?

GOT TO KNOW A FEW AGENTS. GOT WARNED ABOUT THE BOREDOM LEVEL.

OH, C'MON, ROMY... WORSE THAN BEING A COP?

WAY.

FOR EVERY TIME THEY COME WALKING ALL OVER OUR CASES YANKING JURISDICTION, THEY'VE GOT LIKE TWO THOUSAND PIECES OF PAPER THEY HAVE TO FILE BEFOREHAND.

HELL, I CAN BARELY GET MY REPORTS IN ON TIME AS IT IS...

YEAH, ME TOO...

AND IF I WANTED TO SPEND MY DAYS TYPING, I'D'VE JOINED THE I.R.S.

EXCEPT THOSE SCHMUCKS CAN'T CARRY.

$#@%, MARCUS, THEY DON'T NEED TO.

EVENING, MISTER YANCY... I HOPE A DAY IN LOCKUP HAS COOLED YOU OFF.

YOU... YOU'VE GOT NO RIGHT TO KEEP ME HERE.

NO RIGHT.

MOTIVE PART THREE

WRITER **ED BRUBAKER** ARTIST **MICHAEL LARK**

LETTERER **WILLIE SCHUBERT** COLORIST **NOELLE GIDDINGS**

SEPARATOR **LEE LOUGHRIDGE**

ASSISTANT EDITOR **NACHIE CASTRO** EDITOR **MATT IDELSON**

I RENOUNCED MY CITIZENSHIP IN '87.

THE AMERICAN GOVERNMENT'S GOT NO AUTHORITY OVER ME.

WELL, MISTER YANCY, I'M SORRY TO INFORM YOU THAT EVEN NON-CITIZENS LIKE YOURSELF GET THROWN IN JAIL WHEN THEY ATTACK POLICE.

AW, THAT'S BUNK. I DIDN'T KNOW YOU WERE COPS.

BLOOD-ALCOHOL LEVEL AS HIGH AS YOURS LAST NIGHT, I DON'T DOUBT IT.

SO, WHO *DID* YOU THINK WE WERE?

PEOPLE WHO WRECKED MY HOUSE LAST WEEK...

TRYIN' TO DRIVE ME OUT'VE MY *OWN* HOME.

LOCAL YUPPIES DON'T WANT YOU IN THEIR PARK, IS THAT IT?

SCREW WHAT *THEY* WANT.

I GREW UP THERE, THEY JUST SHOWED UP AFTER THE DEVELOPERS RUINED EVERYTHING...

IS THAT WHY YOU KILLED BONNIE LEWIS?

TO GET BACK AT THEM?

WHAT'RE YOU *TALKING* ABOUT?

YOU KNOW, THAT GIRL WHO USED TO BRING YOU FOOD.

HER BRAINS GOT *BASHED* IN LAST THURSDAY NIGHT.

FOUND ONE OF HER LIBRARY BOOKS BURIED IN THE REMAINS OF YOUR HOME.

HEY. HEY... SHE *LENT* ME THAT BOOK.

REALLY?

YEAH, SHE BORROWED BOOKS FOR ME ALL THE TIME.

SHE WASN'T LIKE THE REST OF THEM... SHE UNDERSTOOD MY CAUSE...

YOU GUYS WERE JUST PALS, HUNH?

YEAH, SHE'D BRING ME BOOKS AND FOOD AND STUFF ON HER WAY THROUGH THE PARK. TELL ME ABOUT THE HYPOCRITES SHE WORKED FOR.

SHE HATED THOSE CARPETBAGGING MOTHERS AS MUCH AS I DID.

WHAT ABOUT THE NIGHT OF THE 15TH THAT LAST THURSDAY... DID YOU SEE HER THAT NIGHT?

NO...

SHE WAS SUPPOSED TO PICK UP THAT BOOK ON HER WAY HOME.

BUT SHE NEVER SHOWED UP. I WAITED FOR HER, TOO.

THEN THE NEXT DAY SOME SON OF A B$%*@ SETS MY HOUSE ON FIRE... I SHOULD BE THE ONE FILING THE COMPLAINT HERE...

BUT I SWEAR... I'D NEVER'VE HURT BONNIE...

SHE WAS MY ONLY ALLY.

SO, WHERE DOES THAT LEAVE US?

I DON'T *KNOW*, LIEUTENANT.

SAYS HE'LL TAKE A *POLYGRAPH* IF WE WANT, BUT I'M GUESSIN' HE'LL PASS IT.

STILL HOLDING HIM JUST IN CASE?

YEAH, UNTIL WE DECIDE WHAT TO DO ABOUT THE *ASSAULT* CHARGE.

THIS SUCKS, DETECTIVES.

IT *DOES*.

BUT I JUST DON'T SEE THIS GUY BEING ABLE TO DO THE WHOLE BOGUS EMAIL RANSOM FAX, EITHER.

HE'S JUST SOME KOOK THINKS THE GOVERNMENT'S SCREWING HIM IN THE EAR.

WHAT'S WITH ALL THE LONG FACES?

SOMEBODY *DIE*?

AND THE LOCAL *COMEDIANS* RETURN...

...I HOPE YOU'VE GOT SOME SUNSHINE FOR ME THIS EVENING, SERGEANT.

WE'VE GOT A *STORY*. NOT SURE HOW IT STACKS UP, THOUGH...

SO, THIS FIREBUG SKEL BREAKS *BOTH* ARMS AND A LEG IN HIS LITTLE SWAN DIVE. GOT HIM ALL TRUSSED UP AND UNDER GUARD AT SAINT LUKE'S...

"...BUT HE'S STILL PRETTY COHERENT SO WE GO DOWN TO QUESTION HIM..."

"...AND HE'S ALL HARD-LUCK STORIES..."

--SERIOUS, MAN... JUST LOOK AT ME.

THAT FREAKIN' SUIT RUINED MY LIFE... I ALMOST *DIED.*

AND WHEN WOULD THIS'VE BEEN?

ALMOST TWO YEARS AGO.

MOB DOC SAVED MY HIDE, BUT HE COULDN'T DO ANYTHING ABOUT THE SCARRING...

I COULDN'T EXACTLY *WALTZ* INTO THE E.R. THOUGH, SO WHO WAS I TO COMPLAIN?

WE'RE CERTAINLY IN AGREEMENT YOU'RE AN *UGLY* PIECE OF WORK, JOEY...

"...BUT HOW DOES THAT PROVE YOU'RE NOT OUR PERP ON THESE *ARSON ROBBERIES?*

I DON'T EVEN *HAVE* A FIREBUG SUIT ANYMORE. I SOLD MY BACKUP ONLINE A YEAR AGO.

YOU CAN DO THAT?

JUST SELL YOUR *SUPER-VILLAIN* JUNK ON G-BAY OR SOMEPLACE?

SEEMS LIKE THAT WOULD BE SOME KIND OF A FELONY.

IT'S AN UNDERGROUND AUCTION HOUSE, STARTED OUT OF KEYSTONE CITY.

AND LISTEN, MY MERCH WAS CLEARLY ADVERTISED FOR COLLECTORS ONLY.

LET ME GET THIS STRAIGHT... YOU SOLD YOUR TOTALLY ILLEGAL FLYING ARSON SUIT, BUT IT'S OKAY 'CAUSE YOU SAID IT WAS FOR COLLECTORS ONLY?

YEAH, SOLD IT AS *MEMORABILIA.*

I FOUGHT BATMAN IN THAT SUIT ONCE...

PEOPLE PAY GOOD MONEY FOR THAT.

FOUGHT BATMAN. YEAH, FOR LIKE THREE SECONDS.

MORE'N YOU.

I DON'T NEED TO FIGHT BATMAN, *JERK!*

I GET TO FIGHT MORONS WITH *FREEZE RAYS* AND *FEAR GAS* ALL YEAR LONG.

HEY-- *UKK!*

ALL RIGHT, NATE... EASE OFF.

THAT'S *POLICE BRUTALITY!*

SHUT UP, JOEY, AND LISTEN TO YOUR CHOICES...

YOU CAN EITHER DO HARD TIME FOR SELLING AN ILLEGAL, DANGEROUS WEAPON, OR YOU CAN GIVE UP THE GUY WHO BOUGHT THE SUIT...

PICK ONE.

I DON'T KNOW HIS NAME.

IT WAS A BLIND AUCTION.

GUESS WE CAN'T HELP YOU...

WAIT! WAIT!

I CAN IDENTIFY HIM!

I MET THE GUY ONCE, JUST TO SHOW HIM HOW EVERYTHING *WORKED*...

TO SHOW HIM HOW THE *MEMORABILIA* WORKED?

"...ANYWAY, HE SWEARS ON HIS MOTHER'S GRAVE-- AND SHE'S STILL ALIVE, I *CHECKED*-- THAT THE GUY WHO BOUGHT THE STUPID SUIT IS SOME RICH WHITE GUY."

SO, IT LOOKS LIKE WE'VE GOT SOME NEW *WANNABE* OUT THERE MAKING GOOD.

YOU GOING TO SIT HIM DOWN WITH AN ARTIST?

YEAH, THEY'RE WHEELING HIM IN LATER ON, I THINK.

GOT A GUY COMING BY TO DO A COMP...

WELL, I'M GLAD TO SEE *BOTH* OUR BIGGEST INVESTIGATIONS ARE GETTING NOWHERE.

I CAN HARDLY *WAIT* TO TELL THE COMMISSIONER...

I DIDN'T KNOW BETTER I'D THINK THE PROBE JUST MADE A FUNNY.

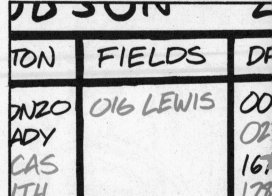

DBSON

TON | FIELDS | DF

ONZO | 016 LEWIS | 00
ADY | | 02
CAS | | 167
TH | | 178

MARCUS...?

WHAT?

IS THIS SUPPOSED TO BE SOME KIND OF SÉANCE OR SOMETHING?

BONNIE LEWIS'S SPIRIT TALKING TO YOU?

IF IT WAS, I'M SURE IT WOULD BE NOTHING BUT COMPLAINTS.

JOB I'VE BEEN DOING ON THIS...

GIVE YOURSELF A BREAK.

A LOT'S HAPPENED SINCE THIS CASE STARTED...

I JUST, I CAN'T HELP THINKING THAT CHARLIE WOULD SEE SOMETHING WE'RE NOT...

IF HE WERE HERE.

CHARLIE FIELDS WAS A GREAT POLICE, MARCUS, BUT EVEN HE COULDN'T MAKE CONNECTIONS WHERE NONE EXIST.

ALL OUR LEADS ON THIS HAVE BEEN NON-STARTERS. IT'S NOT OUR FAULT.

NO, WE'RE MISSING SOMETHING, I KNOW IT.

WHAT?

LOOK-- SOMEONE KILLS BONNIE LEWIS, THEN THEY STASH HER BODY HERE, RIGHT?

I'M WITH YOU SO FAR...

BUT THEN THEY SENT A RANSOM NOTE TO THROW HER FOLKS AND US OFF-TRACK.

I MEAN, IF SHE'D JUST DISAPPEARED, WE'D BE AT LEAST PARTIALLY LOOKING FOR A RANDOM KILLER. BUT THE NOTE MAKES IT OUT TO BE SOMEONE WHO KNEW HER.

OTHERWISE, WHY WORRY ABOUT KEEPING US FROM THINKING SHE'S DEAD?

GIVE THEM TIME TO MAKE SURE ALL THE EVIDENCE IS CLEANED UP.

ESTABLISH A SOLID ALIBI.

RIGHT, AND NOT ONLY DOES EVERYONE HAVE AN ALIBI, BUT AS FAR AS I CAN TELL...

...THERE'S ABSOLUTELY NO MOTIVE FOR THIS MURDER.

BUT THE PROBLEM WITH THE MOTIVELESS CRIME IS THAT THERE'S ALWAYS A MOTIVE...

WE JUST CAN'T SEE IT.

'CAUSE NO ONE KILLS SOMEONE WITH NO REASON.

I MEAN, IT MAY BE BECAUSE THEY WANTED THEIR *SHOES,* OR THEY JUST HAPPENED TO WALK BY WHEN THE PERP SNAPPED...

BUT THERE'S ALWAYS SOME-THING.

WE'RE JUST MISSING THE *SOMETHING.*

SO, THAT'S WHY WE'RE BACK TO SQUARE ONE, *hunh?*

I GUESS... IT'S WHAT *CHARLIE* ALWAYS DID...

WELL, YOU KNOW, TECHNICALLY, THIS IS SQUARE *TWO,* NOT ONE.

WHAT?

SHE WAS *KILLED* SOMEWHERE THEN *DUMPED* HERE. THAT SOMEWHERE IS SQUARE *ONE.*

...SOMEWHERE BETWEEN THE COMBS APARTMENT AND THE PARK...

AW, GOD...

WHAT?

YOU'RE A *GENIUS...*

THIS IS DETECTIVE 12 TO *CENTRAL...* COME IN.

THIS IS CENTRAL.

I NEED TO SPEAK TO SERGEANT DAVIES ASAP...

HEY, MISTER COMBS. THANKS FOR COMING DOWN ON SUCH SHORT NOTICE.

WELL, I HOPE THIS ISN'T GOING TO TAKE LONG, I HAVE AN EARLY MEETING TOMORROW...

JUST NEED YOU TO I.D. OUR PERP, AND I'LL BE OUT OF YOUR HAIR FOR GOOD, HOPEFULLY.

ANYTHING TO HELP, THEN, I SUPPOSE.

JUST RIGHT THROUGH HERE, SIR...

WELL?

HOW'D YOU FIND HIM?

OH, YOU KNOW... MOST POLICE WORK IS JUST BLIND LUCK, JOEY...

SO WHAT DOES THE D.A. THINK? THAT GOOD ENOUGH FOR A WARRANT, AT LEAST?

CALLING THE JUDGE RIGHT NOW...

OKAY, MISTER COMBS, IS ANY OF THESE MEN THE ONE WHO'S BEEN LOITERING IN THE PARK DOWN THE BLOCK FROM YOUR HOME?

YES. NUMBER FOUR.

YOU'RE CERTAIN?

ABSOLUTELY. HE'S BEEN BEGGING CHANGE FROM ME FOR YEARS...

...IS HE THE ONE WHO KILLED BONNIE?

I CAN'T REALLY COMMENT ON THAT, OFFICIALLY...

...BUT JUST BETWEEN YOU AND ME SIR, HE'S GOING DOWN.

ALL RIGHT, MISTER COMBS. I GUESS THAT DOES IT. THANKS FOR YOUR--

ACTUALLY, IF IT'S NOT A PROBLEM, I'D LIKE TO GO OVER ONE MORE THING ABOUT YOUR STATEMENT...?

WELL... HOW LONG IS THIS GOING TO TAKE?

JUST LIKE, TWENTY MINUTES AT THE MOST...

"...I JUST WANT TO MAKE SURE THERE'S NOTHING WE MISSED, IN CASE OF A TRIAL."

WAIT. WAIT A SECOND. MY HUSBAND ISN'T EVEN HERE.

I NEED TO CALL--

YOUR HUSBAND IS TALKING TO THE POLICE RIGHT NOW, MRS. COMBS. HE'S GOING TO BE A WHILE...

BUT-- BUT WHAT ARE YOU LOOKING FOR?

IT'S ON THE WARRANT, MA'AM...

SORRY ABOUT THAT, MISTER COMBS. HAD A POSSIBLE *DEVELOPMENT* ON ANOTHER 'CASE'...

I CAN HARDLY SEE HOW THAT'S ANY REASON TO KEEP ME WAITING NEARLY AN HOUR.

I TOLD YOU ALREADY THAT I--

LISTEN, WE'RE REALLY *SORRY,* HONESTLY.

WE'VE JUST HAD THIS *FIREFLY* GUY UP OUR BUTTS ALL WEEK.

I THOUGHT IT WAS THE *FIREBUG.* WASN'T IT?

IS THAT *RIGHT,* ROMY? FIREFLY OR *BUG?*

I THINK IT *IS* BUG, ACTUALLY.

ANYWAY, THAT'S NEITHER HERE NOR THERE--

ONE WACKO COSTUMED FREAK IS AS GOOD AS *ANOTHER,* RIGHT?

I SUPPOSE SO.

OKAY, LET ME SEE IF I'VE GOT THIS STRAIGHT--

YOUR WIFE AND YOU CAME HOME AROUND 9:00 P.M. THAT THURSDAY, AND BONNIE LEFT SHORTLY AFTER THAT?

THIS IS WHAT YOU WANTED TO GO OVER?

HOW MUCH DID YOU PAY HER THAT NIGHT?

EXCUSE ME?

HOW MUCH DID YOU PAY BONNIE FOR BABY-SITTING THAT NIGHT?

WHY?

IT'S JUST A DETAIL WE NEVER GOT STRAIGHT, THAT'S ALL.

SHE DIDN'T APPEAR TO HAVE BEEN ROBBED, BUT WE DIDN'T FIND ANY MONEY ON HER, SO...

WELL, I CAN'T THINK OFF THE TOP OF MY--

BEEP BEEP

ALARM

WEIRD MESSAGE FOR A BEEPER...

SHOULD LOOK INTO THAT.

YES, IT MUST BE A MISTAKE... I GET PAGED A LOT BY ACCIDENT.

HEY, MARCUS... YOU TAKE A QUICK CALL?

SURE...

HEY MARCUS, GOOD CALL ON THE YUPPIE SCUM...

IT WAS THERE?

YEAH, SOME KIND OF SECRET PANEL IN THE BACK OF HIS CLOSET. ALMOST MISSED IT.

FIND ANYTHING CONCLUSIVE YET?

GOT RESIDUE ON ONE OF HIS ANTIGRAV TANKS.

C.S.U.'S DOING A P.C.R. AS WE SPEAK.

--YOUR WIFE SAID YOU *BOTH* WALKED HER DOWN TO THE DOOR?

BUT WOULDN'T ONE OF YOU STAY WITH YOUR SON?

HE'S NOT AN INFANT.

OH, I'M SURE, IT'S JUST--

SORRY ABOUT THAT. EVERYTHING SEEMS TO BE WRAPPING UP, I GUESS.

WHAT DO YOU MEAN?

WELL, I HAD *MOST* OF IT FIGURED OUT, SIR...

I JUST DIDN'T KNOW HOW *YOU* KNEW BONNIE'D BEEN SNOOPING AROUND IN YOUR CLOSET.

WHAT ARE YOU *TALKING* ABOUT?

IT SEEMS BONNIE LIKED TO DIG THROUGH HER CUSTOMER'S STUFF. A REAL NOSEY LITTLE KID.

BUT YOU KNOW THAT, DON'T YOU? 'CAUSE SHE DISCOVERED YOUR SECRET.

I DON'T KNOW WHAT YOU'RE TALKING ABOUT, AND I WANT TO LEAVE NOW.

THAT BEEPER MESSAGE OF YOURS THAT JUST WENT OFF? THAT WAS BECAUSE ONE OF OUR DETECTIVES JUST POPPED THE SECRET DOOR OUT OF YOUR CLOSET, TOO.

SET OFF A SILENT ALARM WHICH GOES RIGHT TO YOUR PAGER.

SMART PLAN, REALLY.

IT'S SORT OF PATHETIC, THOUGH, TOO, ISN'T IT?

THE PEOPLE WHO DIED SO YOU COULD PROTECT YOUR SECRET IDENTITY?

I MEAN WE'VE GOT BONNIE LEWIS, WHOSE HEAD YOU BASHED IN WITH ONE OF YOUR ANTI-GRAV TANKS-- ACCORDING TO C.S.U. AT LEAST...

...AND THEN THERE'S MY PARTNER CHARLIE FIELDS, WHO DIED FOLLOWING UP A LEAD ON YOUR BOGUS KIDNAPPING.

THAT-- THAT WASN'T MY FAULT.

I DIDN'T... NO--

YOU TRICKED ME!

YOU DIDN'T READ ME MY RIGHTS! AND YOU TRICKED ME!

SCREW YOUR RIGHTS.

WE'VE GOT YOUR WIFE TALKIN' A MILE A MINUTE, RIGHT NOW. WE'VE GOT THE FIREBUG SUIT, AND WE'VE GOT BONNIE'S BLOOD ON YOUR TANK.

YOU
CAN'T-
YOU--

I CAN'T
TELL YOU
HOW MUCH
I WAS
HOPING
YOU'D TRY
THAT...

"I MUST SAY... THE NIGHT *HAS* BEEN KIND TO US, DETECTIVES...

"... THIS WAS DAMN FINE WORK FOR *ALL* OF YOU.

"THE COMMISSIONER'LL BE *VERY* PLEASED."

I'M *OKAY* WITH PLEASED, BUT I'LL BE *HAPPIER* IF THERE'S A *BONUS,* TOO.

DON'T GET YOUR HOPES UP, SERGEANT...

BUT I *WILL* SIGN OFF ON YOU ALL TAKING AN *EARLY NIGHT* TO *CELEBRATE...*

I *GUESS* THAT'LL HAVE TO DO... *TINO'S,* EVERYONE?

SOUNDS GOOD TO ME. WHERE'D *DRIVER* DISAPPEAR TO...?

"...IT'S *HIS* BIG NIGHT."

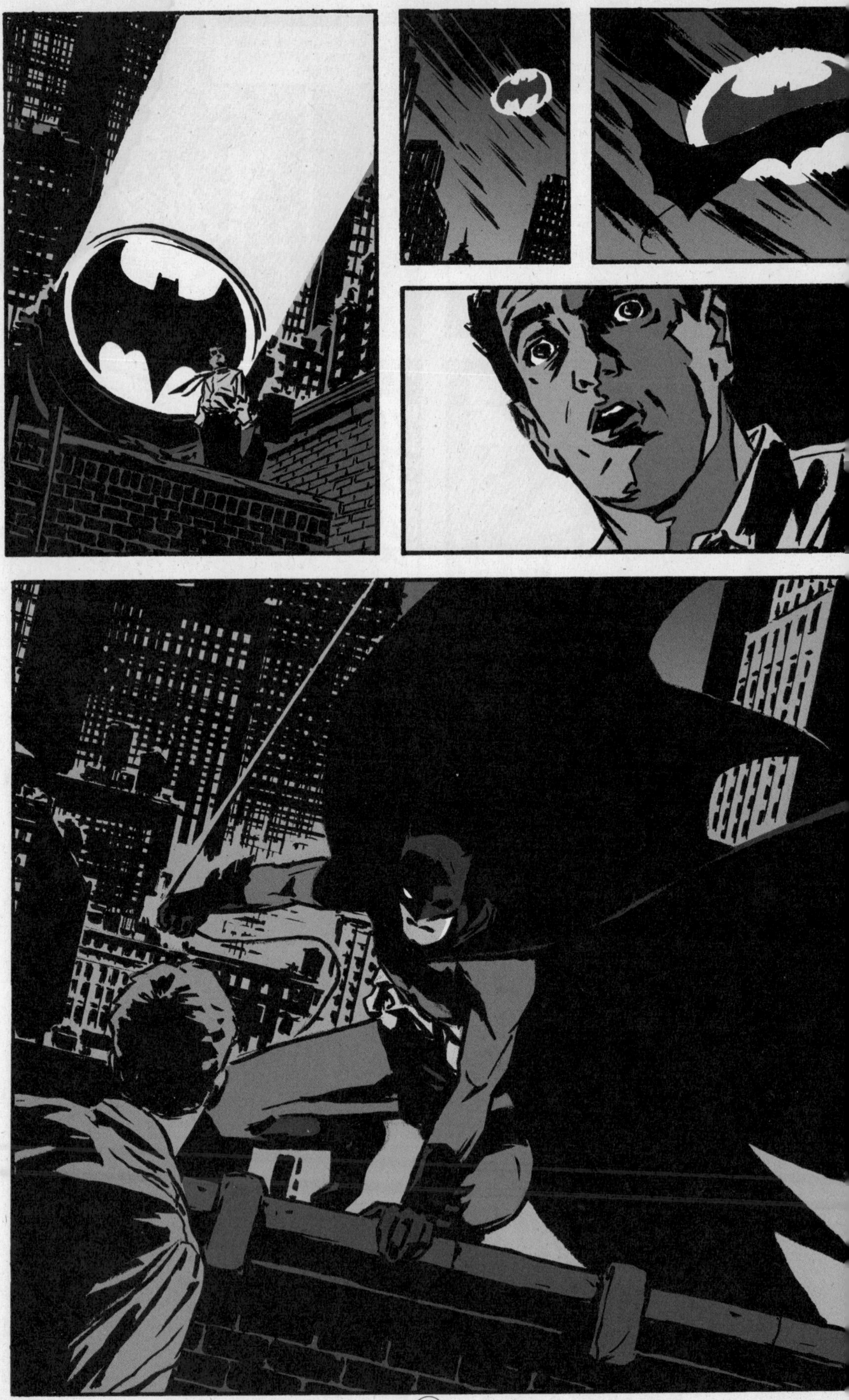

DETECTIVE DRIVER?

WHAT IS IT?

I JUST WANT YOU TO KNOW THAT WE TOOK DOWN THAT FIREBUG FREAK TONIGHT.

AND WE DID IT ALONE, WITHOUT YOUR HELP.

GOOD.

THANK YOU.

THAT'S ALL YOU'VE GOT TO SAY? A GOOD COP DIED BECAUSE OF THESE FREAKIN' NUTJOBS THAT JUST CRAWL OUT OF THE WOODWORK IN THIS GODFORSAKEN TOWN...

...AND THAT'S ALL YOU'VE GOT TO SAY?

NO, IT'S NOT...

DON'T USE THAT SIGNAL AGAIN UNLESS IT'S AN EMERGENCY.

I'M SORRY ABOUT DETECTIVE FIELDS, BUT I'VE GOT WORK TO DO.

KLIK

ARE YOU INSANE...?

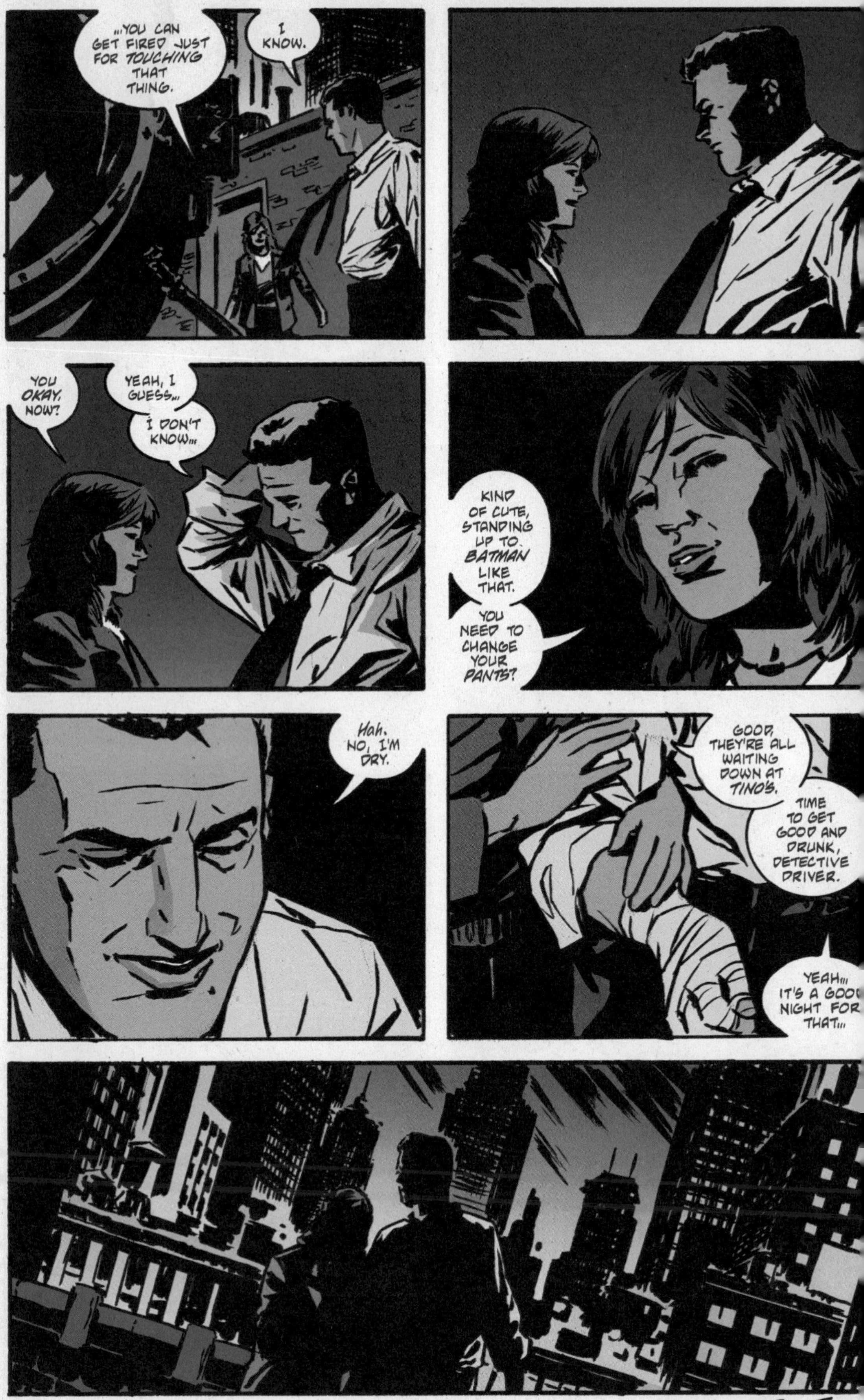
...YOU CAN GET FIRED JUST FOR *TOUCHING* THAT THING.
I KNOW.
YOU *OKAY,* NOW?
YEAH, I GUESS...
I DON'T KNOW...
KIND OF CUTE, STANDING UP TO *BATMAN* LIKE THAT.
YOU NEED TO CHANGE YOUR *PANTS?*
Hah. NO, I'M DRY.
GOOD, THEY'RE ALL WAITING DOWN AT *TINO'S.*
TIME TO GET GOOD AND DRUNK, DETECTIVE DRIVER.
YEAH... IT'S A GOOD NIGHT FOR THAT...
THE END

COVER GALLERY

ART BY MICHAEL LARK · COLOR BY NOELLE GIDDINGS · SEPARATED BY DIGITAL CHAMELEON

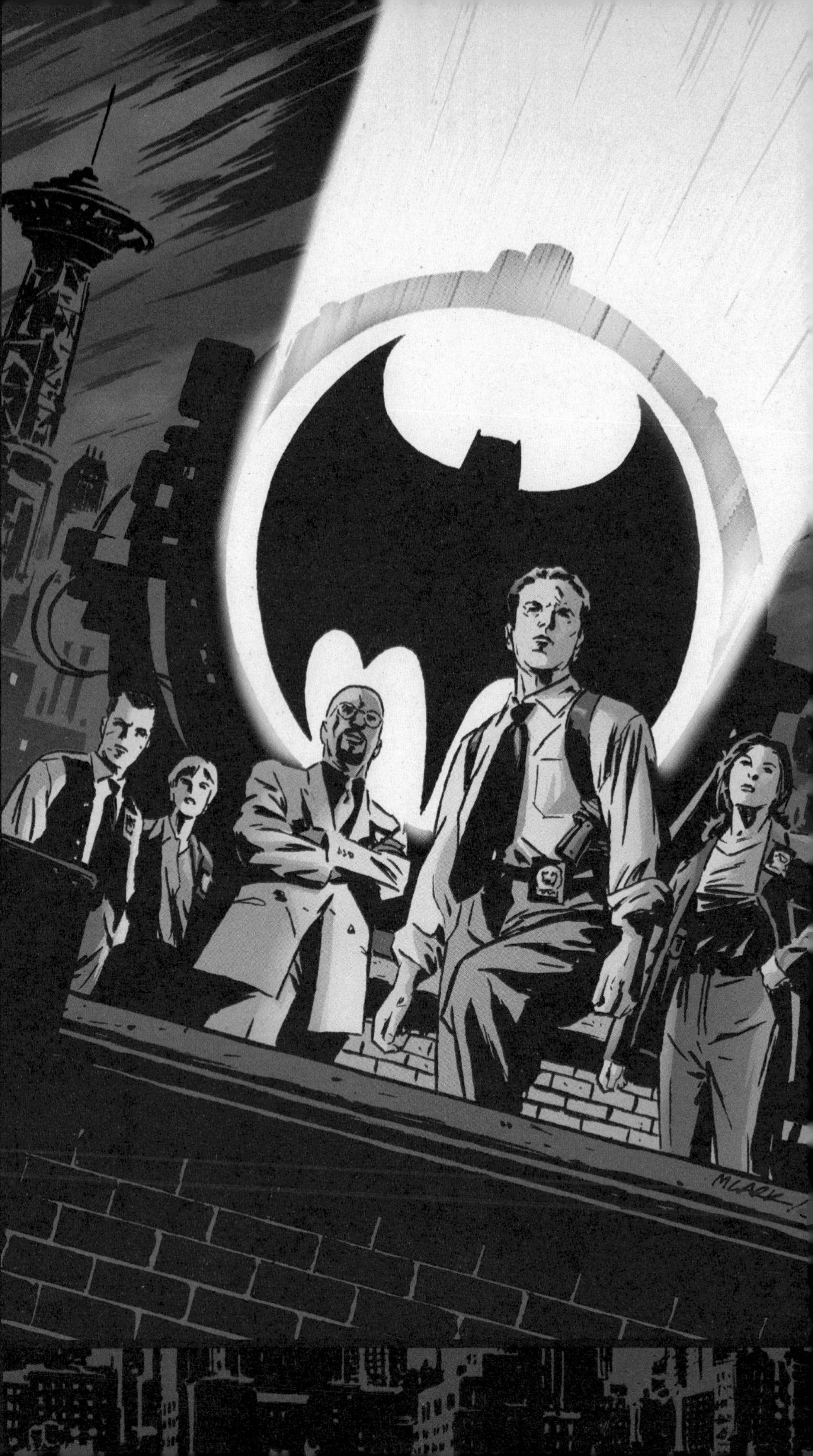

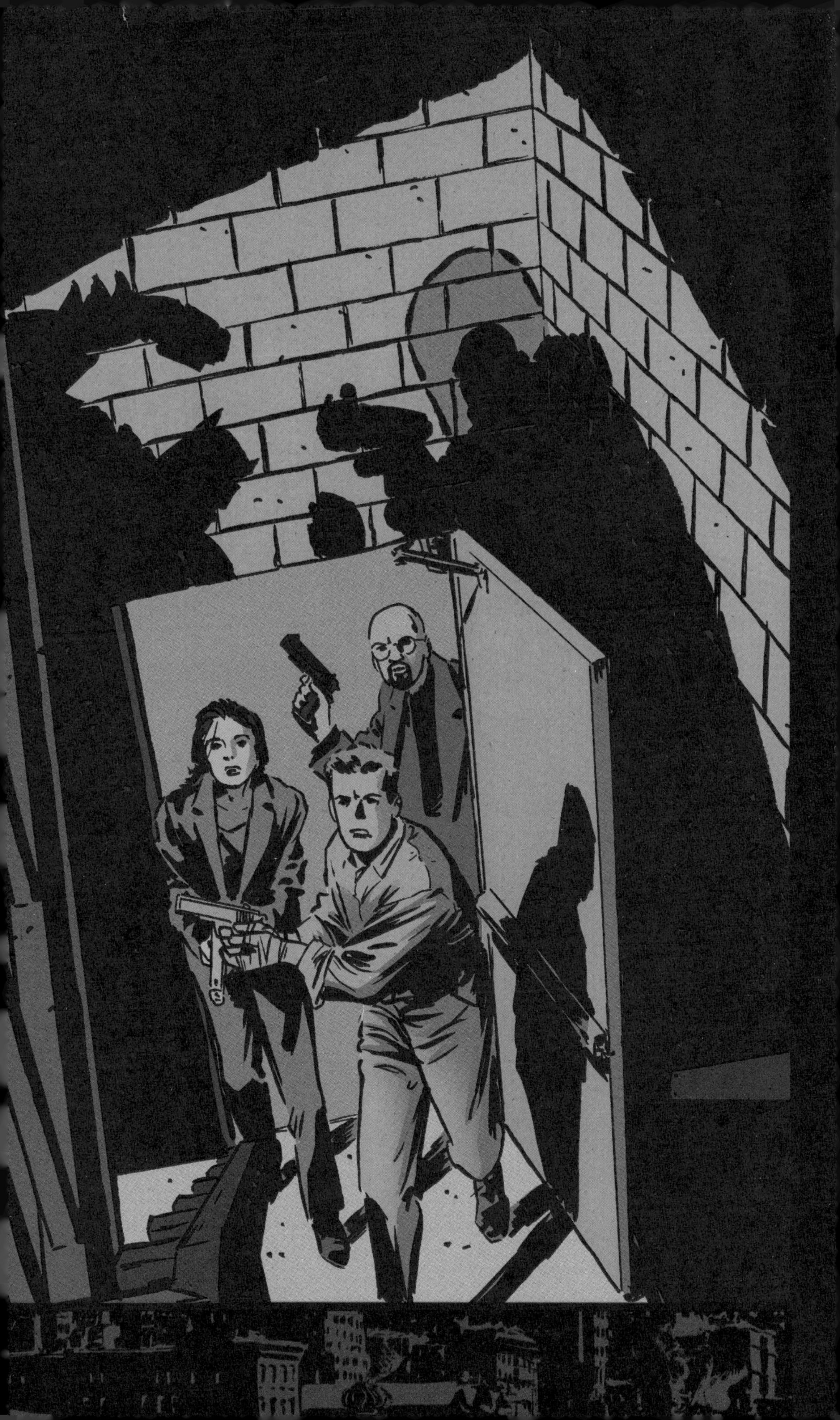

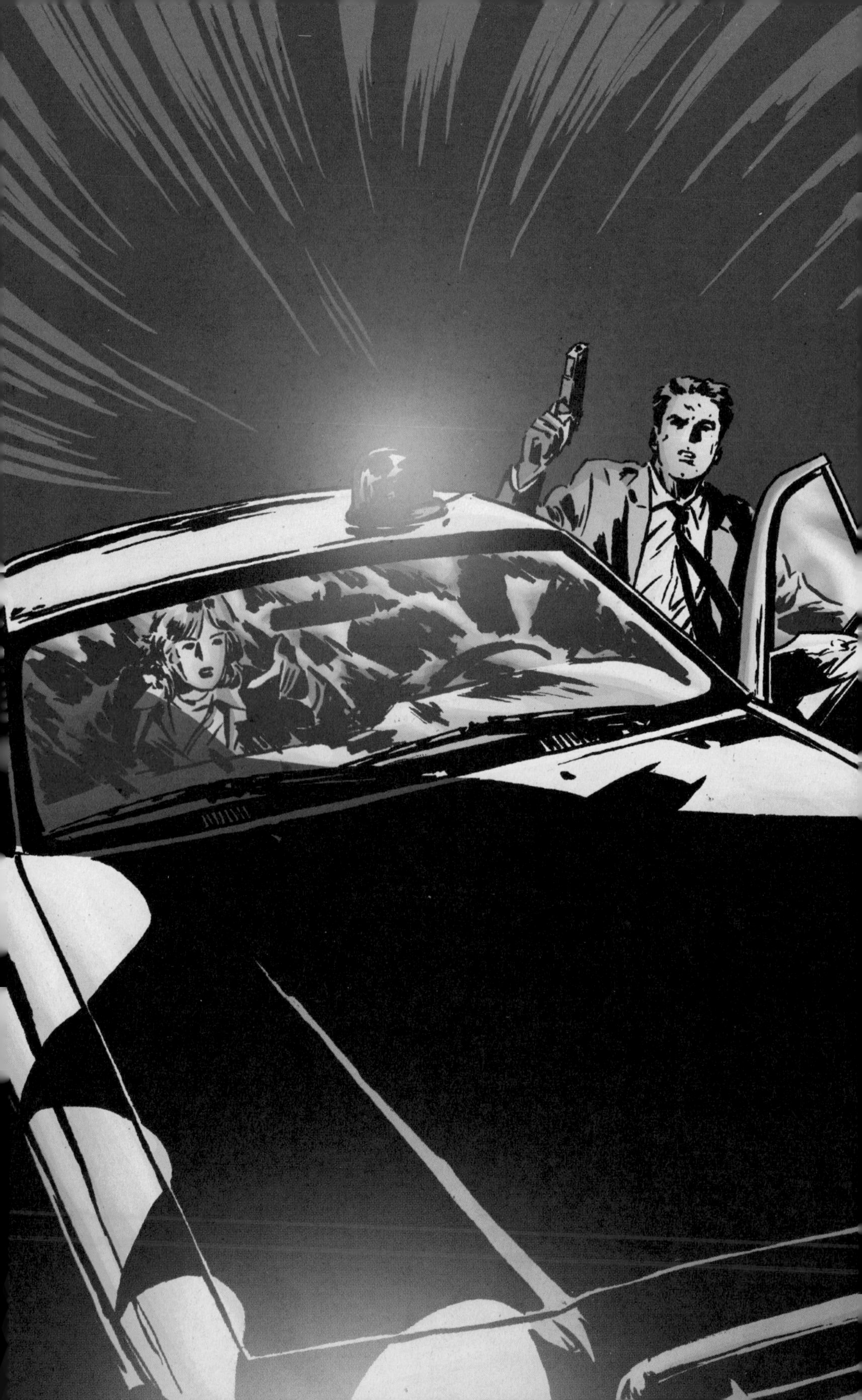

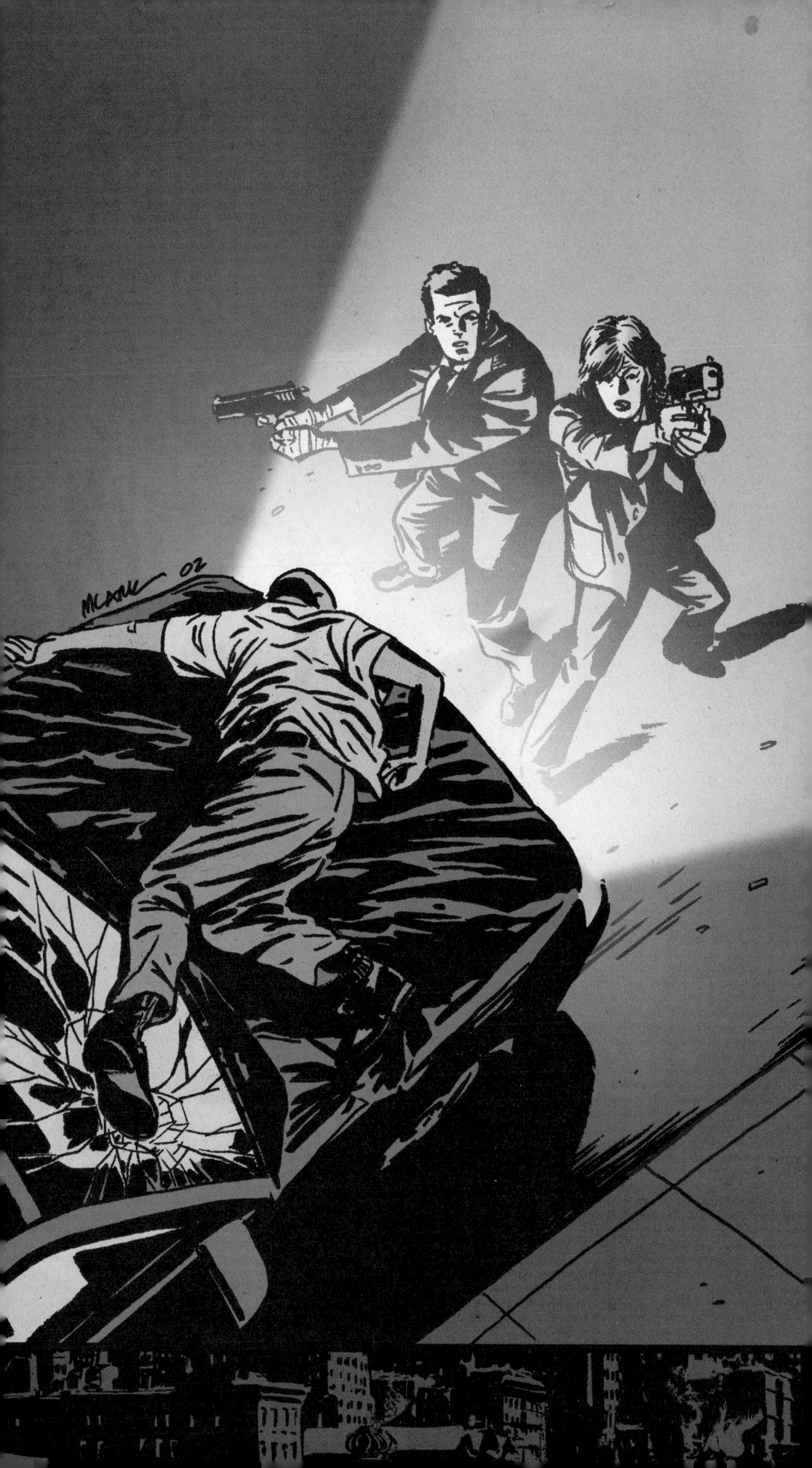

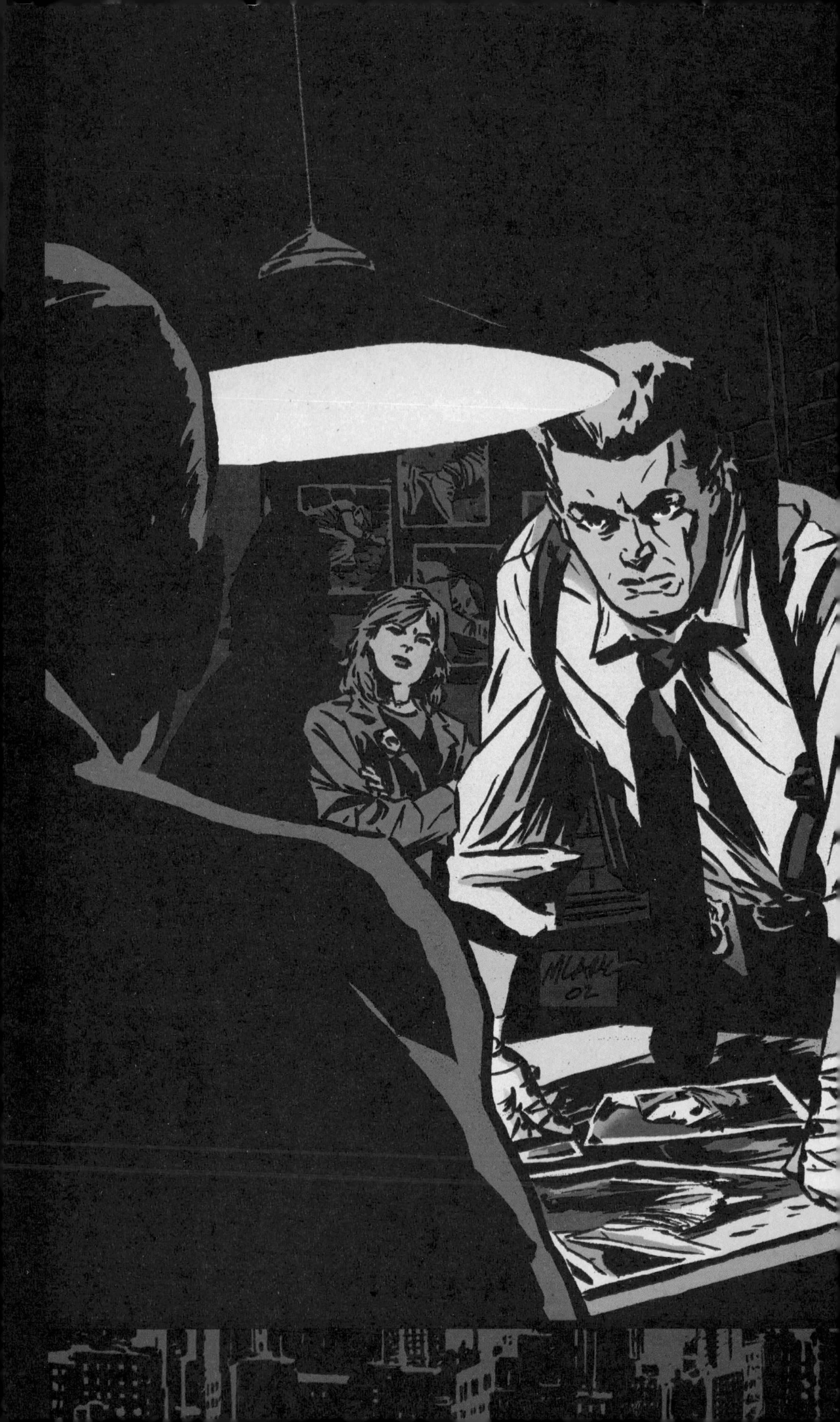

MARKER ROUGHS OF A PAGE FROM ISSUE #4.

STAFFING THE GCPD

In defining the approach to producing GOTHAM CENTRAL in tandem, writers Greg Rucka and Ed Brubaker divided the cast into the day and night shifts, each masterminding one twelve-hour block. They prepared extensive notes on each of the detectives and uniformed officers for artist Michael Lark. Michael's character designs for the cast are on the following pages.

DETAILED CONCEPT SKETCH
OF THE MCU SQUADROOM.

JACKSON DAVIES

NELSON CROWE

ROMY
CHANDLER

NATE
PATTON

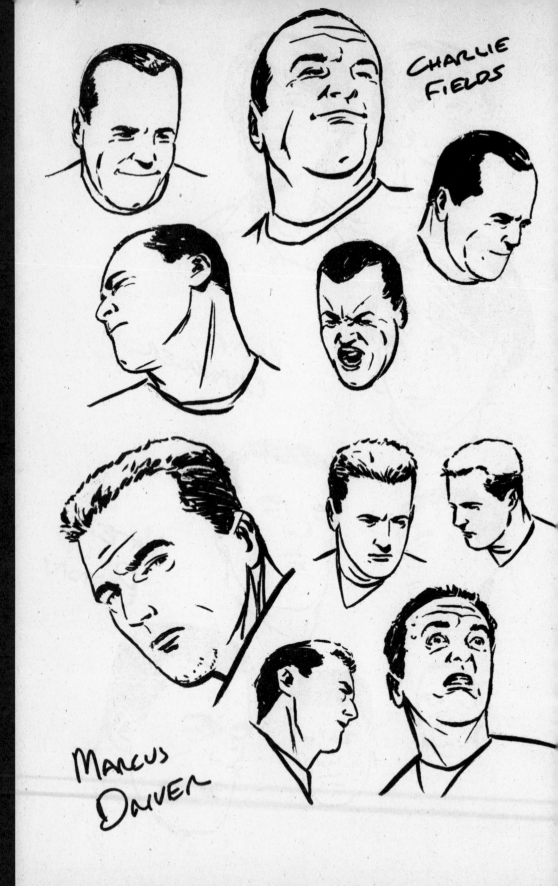

CHARLIE
FIELDS

MARCUS
DRIVER

FIGURE STUDIES FOR
THE COVER OF ISSUE #5.

BATMAN
THE QUEST FOR JUSTICE CONTINUES IN THESE BOOKS FROM DC: